PENGUIN BOOKS

BREAST-FEEDING
AND NATURAL CHILD SPACING

After her graduation as a dental hygienist from
the University of California Medical Center in
San Francisco, Sheila Kippley married and
began raising a family. She became interested
in breast-feeding following the birth of her
first child. A few years later, when her husband's work had taken her to Canada, she
started a La Leche League group, whose
members often questioned her about breast-
feeding and its relationship to child spacing.
As a result she began collecting material to
help mothers and eventually wrote *Breast-
Feeding and Natural Child Spacing*. In the
fall of 1971 she and her husband founded the
Couple to Couple League, which helps couples
to learn the art of natural family planning.
Mrs. Kippley is the mother of four children.

Breast-Feeding and Natural Child Spacing

The Ecology of Natural Mothering

Sheila Kippley

Drawings by Gigi Nealon

Penguin Books

Penguin Books Ltd, Harmondsworth,
Middlesex, England
Penguin Books, 625 Madison Avenue,
New York, New York 10022, U.S.A.
Penguin Books Australia Ltd, Ringwood,
Victoria, Australia
Penguin Books Canada Limited, 2801 John Street,
Markham, Ontario, Canada L3R 1B4
Penguin Books (N.Z.) Ltd, 182–190 Wairau Road,
Auckland 10, New Zealand

First published in the United States of America by
Harper & Row, Publishers, Inc., 1974
Published in Penguin Books by arrangement with
Harper & Row, Publishers, Inc., 1975
Reprinted 1976, 1977, 1978, 1979, 1980, 1982

Printed in the United States of America by
Kingsport Press, Inc., Kingsport, Tennessee
Set in Times Roman

Grateful acknowledgment is hereby made to the following to reprint the
material specified:

Excerpt from "The Effect of Breast-feeding on the Rate of Conception"
by Dr. Christopher Tietze. Reprinted by permission of the author.
Excerpt from article "About Pacifiers" by Margaret Abler, from the
May–June 1972 issue of *Leaven*. Reprinted by permission of La Leche
League International and the author.
Excerpt from *The Absorbent Mind* by Maria Montessori. Translated by
Claude A. Claremont. Reprinted by permission of Holt, Rinehart &
Winston, Inc.
Excerpt from *How to Raise a Human Being* by Lee Salk and Rita
Kramer. Copyright © 1969 by Lee Salk and Rita Kramer. Reprinted
by permission of Random House, Inc.
Excerpt from the November–December 1972 issue of *LLL News*. Reprinted
by permission of La Leche League International.
Excerpt from "The Cultural Warping of Childbirth" by Doris Haire. Re-
printed by permission of the author.

(*continued*)

Excerpt from "Maternal Nutrition and Child Health," Publication 123, Food and Nutrition Board, National Academy of Sciences–National Research Council, Washington, D.C., November 1950.

Excerpt from *Brennemann's Practice of Pediatrics: Breast-Feeding and Mixed Feeding* by Lee Forrest Hill, M.D. Reprinted by permission of Medical Department, Harper & Row, Publishers, Inc.

Excerpt from article "How I Get Mothers To Breast Feed" by Dr. Kimball, from the June 1968 issue of *Physician's Management*. Reprinted by permission of *Physician's Management*.

Excerpt from article by Virginia Beal, from *Pediatrics*, Vol. 20. Reprinted by permission of American Academy of Pediatrics and the author.

Excerpt from *Abreast of the Times* by Dr. Richard Applebaum. Reprinted by permission of the author.

Excerpt from "The Uniqueness of Human Milk," from the *American Journal of Clinical Nutrition 24*. Published 1971. Reprinted by permission of the Federation of American Societies for Experimental Biology.

Excerpt from *The Nursing Mother* by Frank Howard Richardson. Published by Prentice-Hall, Inc., Englewood Cliffs, N.J.

Excerpt from *Childbirth Without Fear* by Grantly Dick-Read. Reprinted by permission of Harper & Row, Publishers, Inc.

Excerpt from *How Do Your Children Grow?* by Eda LeShan. Copyright © 1972 by Eda J. LeShan, published by David McKay Company, Inc., and reprinted by permission of the publisher.

Excerpt from *The Child Under Six* by James Hymes, Jr. © 1961, 1963 by James Hymes, Jr. Published by Prentice-Hall, Inc., Englewood Cliffs, N.J.

Excerpt from "Report on Breastfeeding and Amenorrhea," from *Marriage and Family Newsletter*, March 1972. Reprinted by permission of *Marriage and Family Newsletter*.

Excerpt from article by Dr. Otto Schaefer, from the December 1971 issue of *Nutrition Today*. Reprinted by permission of *Nutrition Today*.

"Of Babies, Beds and Teddy Bears" reprinted by permission of *Marriage* magazine.

Editor's reply from *JAMA*, Vol. 167, May 3, 1958. Reprinted by permission of the *Journal of the American Medical Association*.

Acknowledgments

This book could not have been written in its present form without the help of others. Thus I want to thank all of the publishers who graciously gave me permission to quote from their publications as noted throughout the text. The many mothers who told me their experiences either personally or by mail made an invaluable contribution to the writing of this book. To each of them I express my deep thanks. Many readers will recognize that I have been influenced by La Leche League. I freely and gratefully acknowledge my great debt to that organization, and I certainly thank those League members and officials who have helped me in various ways. Lastly, I want to express my gratitude to my husband, who first suggested that I breast-feed our babies. His aid in preparing the manuscript was indeed significant.

Contents

Foreword

As the title of the book indicates, ecology is complicated. Environmentalists are becoming more aware that actions which affect one aspect of nature frequently have effects which are far more widespread than previously suspected. The recent interest in ecology has centered primarily upon the effects that man's actions have had in the subhuman world of rivers, plants, and animals. Too little attention has been directed to human ecology. In this book, Sheila Kippley makes a real contribution to human ecology by directing attention to the importance of breast-feeding, mothering, and natural birth regulation.

In lay language, her book presents recent biological research studies documenting new biochemical, anti-infective, emotional, and economic advantages of human milk as the ideal food for infants.

Human attitudes are changing, and an increasing number of concerned young people are seeking a more natural and less artificial way of life. Many practices uncritically adopted by modern man are being reappraised. Few people in Western countries realize that the large-scale change from breast-feeding to bottle-feeding has taken place insidiously within the last few generations. Artificial feeding of infants has become so easy and apparently successful that the importance of breast-feeding has not been appreciated.

Most obstetricians, pediatricians, nutritionists, and other health workers have received only superficial information concerning the importance of breast-feeding. The textbooks in current use for the various health professions contain minimal references relating to the anatomy and psychophysiology of breast-feeding. Consequently, those who should be most knowledgeable about the subject are ill prepared by education or experience to advise and educate parents in this regard.

Mrs. Kippley also suggested that I comment on another critical aspect of human ecology, which is not included in her book. That is the nutritional status of the mother during pregnancy. For the first nine months of life (intrauterine), the infant requires a well-nourished mother. Human and animal studies are accumulating evidence that poor nutritional status of the mother is a very important factor in maternal illness, fetal deaths, prematurity, new-born deaths, and illnesses during infancy.

Three groups of pregnant women are especially vulnerable to poor nutritional status: adolescents who are not prepared for the added stress of pregnancy, women who have always been under-nourished, and older women with poor dietary habits who have become depleted by repeated pregnancies in rapid succession. Diets of pregnant women usually do not differ conspicuously, except in quantity, from their lifetime diets unless the mother is receiving and accepts intensive health guidance. Young adolescent girls comprise a very vulnerable group as they are not ready physically or emotionally to assume the grave responsibilities of motherhood. Before assuming family responsibilities, girls should be educated women, and boys should be mature men capable of supporting a family.

Many influences have gradually crept into our ways of living to sway the mother from breast-feeding her baby. Hospitalization for childbirth usually has been accompanied by a substantial decline in breast-feeding. More often than they know, doctors and nurses promote artificial feeding by their advice, for example, by advocating too early and excessive amounts of solid foods which decrease the mother's production of human milk. In areas of the world where breast-feeding is common, solid foods of questionable quality are fed too late and in insufficient amounts whereas in areas of the world where bottle-feeding is practiced, solid foods are introduced too early and in excessive amounts.

On the basis of extensive scientific studies, all informed physicians agree that milk from a healthy mother meets all the nutritional needs of a full-term healthy infant in the early months of life. However, it should be stressed that limited and selected amounts of solid foods should be fed to thriving infants after about the fifth month of life. A few teaspoonsful of ripe banana is very easy to mash and give for the infant's first solid food. An egg yolk also is simple to prepare and can be fed with the banana to provide a very nutritious supplement rich in iron. As the baby grows, one to two tablespoonsful of precooked baby cereal (fortified with iron) also can be given with warm water. Well-cooked and finely sieved legume (beans, peas) can be used to replace the egg yolk if the latter is too expensive for the family. After six months it is desirable to include limited amounts of sieved vegetables and fruits to provide variety in flavor and texture as well as other essential nutrients.

Mrs. Kippley's book also presents the scientific evidence documenting that lactation, besides providing the safest and the most economical source of nutrients for the infant, is also of major importance in decreasing the birth rate. Accumulated demographic data from birth records all over the world indicate that the average spacing of children is about every two years if the mother's milk supplies the major source of calories for her baby during the first twelve to eighteen months of life. Controlled clinical studies show that lactation does prolong postpartum amenorrhea and that conception during this time is very low. Of course, everyone knows of someone who became pregnant while nursing. The information that Sheila Kippley shares in this book is to define the conditions which are most likely to provide an extended period of postpartum natural infertility; she distinguishes these sharply from the token breast-feeding of contemporary Western culture. She also indicates the symptoms of the return of fertility. The author is rightly quite concerned to stress that the birth control aspect of breast-feeding is a side effect that comes from doing what is best for the baby.

On the basis of extensive clinical experience, it is my opinion that to establish a stable happy family, it is desirable for couples to have children during the early years of married life and later to limit the size of the family in keeping with their resources. The use of symptothermic family planning on a couple-to-couple basis is a movement which is gaining momentum throughout the world. This natural, safe, and free method requires education and motivation of the husband and wife, but can be very effective in controlling the size of the family. The father should assume at least equal responsibility with his wife in controlling the size of the family.

Since economic survival in underdeveloped agricultural communities may depend upon the contribution of children both during childhood and as adults, large families appear to be a necessity in areas with a high infant mortality rate and more primitive agricultural methods. Motivation for birth control depends upon the demonstration to such families that infant mortality can be reduced by improved public health programs and that food production can be increased by more efficient agricultural methods. Couples with limited economic resources will become motivated to limit the size of their families as soon as they understand that most of their children will survive and that their social security will be more dependent on how well they provide for and educate their children rather than how many children they have.

The impact of Western nutrition technology is both good and bad. Only recently is attention being directed to consider possible consequences of poorly understood technological changes. It seems especially important to consider the question of infant feeding in this context. In recent years, there is an increasing realization that the delivery of health services to families has developed with little understanding of biological and emotional needs. Ecology concerns not only communities and nations but also the basic "primary unit" of society, that is the family.

As an older, experienced pediatrician and as a grandparent, I recommend this book with enthusiasm to the youth who are seeking a more natural way of life and also to my colleagues in the health professions.

Advances in scientific knowledge have occurred at a rate faster than our ability to apply them effectively for the welfare of man. Every child has the right to be "well born" and to be "well raised." We already can foresee ways to attain this goal ultimately. However, solutions must reach deep into underlying problems of social and economic stability as well as into changes in human attitudes. An ever-increasing number of educated, dedicated people is needed to teach their children, as well as children of the deprived segments of the population, how to live with dignity and to adjust the size of their families within their ability to care for them and to provide for better education for each succeeding generation of children. Therefore, responsible parenthood should include deliberate and generous decisions by some couples with ample resources to have and raise larger families as well as deliberate and generous decisions by couples with more limited resources to restrict the number of their children. The present trend is in the opposite direction and needs to be reversed.

ROBERT L. JACKSON, M.D.
Professor of Pediatrics
University of Missouri
School of Medicine

Introduction

This manual is a book of its times. A hundred years ago it would have been superfluous because breast-feeding was the general practice, and it would have been impossible because of the lack of research at that time. Today, however, I hope it fills a need.

The book grew out of a great many conversations I had with other mothers who shared with me a common interest in providing our babies with the benefits of breast-feeding and in securing the additional side effect of child spacing. All of us ran up against what seemed to be a nearly universal skepticism about both of these common interests—at least at the level of housewife hearsay. On the other hand, at the level of medical research, our common interests were bolstered. When I frequently found myself playing the role of transmitter of scientific information about breast-feeding and child spacing, I decided that there was a general knowledge gap on the part of many mothers and doctors that might be narrowed by a book of this type.

More importantly, the methods advocated in this manual provided a double service to friends of mine who had previously been unsuccessful in their earlier attempts at breast-feeding. First of all, they became successful nursing mothers and, as a result, came to a greater enjoyment of their babies. Secondly, they experienced a form of child spacing for which they were not only appreciative, but which some of them had believed could not be achieved through nursing.

The particular information that I as well as others found needed clarification was the possibility of becoming pregnant while nursing. I came to the realization that some mothers who sincerely wanted to continue to breast-feed their babies were weaning at a very early date for fear of a pregnancy following soon after childbirth. Some of these fears were real because of cultural interference with natural breast-feeding; others were based simply on their doctor's word; almost all were the result of inadequate information. I found that a review of the medical research in this area, plus the adoption of the breast-feeding and child-care program described in this manual, gave some mothers of my acquaintance confidence, peace of mind, and the enjoyment of continued nursing.

I want to stress at the outset that breast-feeding is far more than a merely biological function. It is frequently an emotional experience for both mother and baby; it is truly interpersonal. The breast-feeding mother is not just fulfilling a mammary function; she is also contributing to the personal fulfillment of herself as a mother and to the emotional security and development of her baby. This is part of what is meant by "the ecology of natural mothering," a theme that runs throughout this book.

This is not a book on birth control as such, although I fully realize that some may be interested in what is said here only from the point of view of finding an efficient means of child spacing that meets the moral criteria of everyone. It is not within the scope of this book to delve deeply into a value discussion; rather, the purpose here is to show that, for whatever reason breast-feeding is used, it can be an effective means of spacing children. I will say, however, that the more the mother thinks in terms of doing what is most in accord with nature and what is best for her baby, the more easily she will be able to carry out the program outlined here

Furthermore, it is somewhat doubtful whether the mother who would look at breast-feeding only as a means of birth control would be able to sustain the criticism she might get from her well-meaning friends and advisers. And one doesn't become a member of the smart set by breast-feeding, although some extremely smart women are doing it. Breast-feeding entails a loving personal relationship between mother and baby, and I wonder if the mother who looked upon her suckling baby primarily as a birth-control device would be able to maintain that nursing relationship of love for very long. Psychological studies have indicated that a baby can sense his mother's attitude toward him from the way in which she nurses him,[1] and no one would want to see such a naturally loving relationship distorted. For the mother who may start out with a poor attitude toward her child, however, I can only offer the opinion that, with a little bit of self-giving, there is a much greater chance of her growing to accept, love, and appreciate that baby through breast-feeding than through the use of such artifacts as bottles, formulas, messy baby foods, and pacifiers.

I hope that no one will take offense at my efforts to paraphrase the Man from Nazareth. Speaking of the relationship of secular values and the kingdom of God, He said, "Seek first the kingdom of God and all these other things will be given unto you." What I have been trying to say is that, by seeking first to do what is in accord with God's natural plan, other benefits will follow.

In summary, this book has been written so that mothers, and whoever else is interested, may know about some of the research that has been done concerning breast-feeding and natural infertility and may learn what is meant by natural mothering, as well as its many advantages for the individual baby and mother and its normal effect of child spacing. I hope that many other mothers will come to enjoy the same satisfying relationship with their babies that I have experienced. I hope that they will also, if that is what they want, come to enjoy the derivative effect of natural child spacing.

1. Readers will notice that I have invariably referred to the baby as masculine. This is no subtle longing for a male child (we have four girls), but simply a literary expedient. Many sentences and paragraphs talk about both the mother and baby, and it was much easier to keep the pronouns straight by referring to the baby as he, him, and his.

Some Important Addresses

The following organizations are frequently referred to in the text:

La Leche League International (LLLI)
9616 Minneapolis Avenue
Franklin Park, Ill. 60131
Counseling telephone number at any time: 312 455-7730

ICEA Secretary
P.O. Box 5852
Milwaukee, Wis. 53220

ICEA Supplies Center
1414 N.W. 85th Street
Seattle, Wash. 98117

ICEA Bookcenter
P.O. Box 20048
Minneapolis, Minn. 55420

1

Your Baby's Sucking Needs

THE BREAST FOR NOURISHMENT

One of the baby's strongest needs is the need to suck—and rightly so, for it is the sucking that provides him with nourishment. The sucking of the infant stimulates the production of milk in the mother, and is the natural means of transmitting the milk from mother to baby.

Lactation, or the production of milk in the mother's body, is influenced proportionately by the amount of stimulation the breast receives. This stimulation is most frequently caused by the sucking of the infant. (Another source of stimulation that is not as strong as that caused by the infant is expression of milk by hand or pump.) The more stimulation the breast receives the more milk it will supply or produce. The exact opposite is likewise true. When a baby is weaned naturally from the breast or is weaned by his mother, who introduces foods or formula so that the baby requires less from the breast, then the supply of milk is lessened accordingly. Lactation is a delicate process, for the supply of milk almost always meets the demand, whether that demand is great or small.

The following story illustrates how the mother's milk supply is influenced largely by the baby's demand at the breast. A friend introduced solids early, at the advice of her doctor. Unlike her previous doctor, this new doctor insisted on solids at six weeks, even though he strongly approved of breast-feeding. As soon as she followed his instructions her milk supply decreased, she became depressed, and menstruation returned. Several months later a letter came, telling me that her supply had increased.

Of course, I'm still nursing Jeff. He only has solids once a day. Frank and I both felt we should cut down on solids, and we had a good chance to do so over the Easter holidays when we traveled to Salt Lake. He had very little extra, and I feel this brought back or brought on more milk. Makes me happier.

It is amazing at first to learn how effective the demand for milk can be in producing the supply. There are mothers who want to bring back their milk several months after childbirth because their babies have reacted unfavorably to formulas. With proper instruction and loads of encouragement, these mothers have brought back their milk supply and have been able to breast-feed their babies.

The same process can likewise assist the mother who, worried at first about an insufficient milk supply and deciding the baby perhaps needs a supplement via a bottle, would like to eliminate that supplementary bottle. By doubling or tripling the number of nursings at the breast for one or two days, the mother will usually have plenty of milk, and there will be no further need to use the bottle.

Another example is the mother who has a premature or sick baby. She may express her milk regularly to maintain a supply until her baby comes home. Over a period of six weeks one mother expressed her milk into a sterile jar, which she took daily to the hospital to nourish her premature, incubator baby. Her supply increased from one and one-half ounces to over twenty ounces per day during this period. She met up with much resistance at first, and everyone thought that it wasn't possible. At a later date the pediatrician told her to wean the baby to a bottle by six months of age, the reason given being that the nursing wouldn't do her or the baby any good. Being well read on the subject of breast-feeding, she ignored this advice and both she and the baby prospered.

The relationship between the sucking stimulus and the production of milk is probably best illustrated by the few mothers who have simulated the sucking stimulation in order to produce milk for the baby they planned to adopt. I have corresponded with one mother who actually was producing milk prior to adoption. In another case the mother had not recently given birth; she was without any supply of milk and she was without the normal hormonal and physiological changes of late pregnancy that provide for an adequate and easy milk supply after childbirth. She was, so to speak, bone dry, yet she persevered and developed a milk supply for her adopted baby.

Needless to say, such a process isn't recommended to just anybody, for it takes a considerable amount of constant effort and a very strong desire to nurse one's baby. In addition, it takes a baby who is agreeable to the idea, for, by the time an adoptive mother receives her baby, the infant has already been bottle-fed for several weeks. It takes stronger sucking to get milk from the breast than from the bottle, and some babies are not particularly disposed toward making the transition.[1]

Nature also provides an ample supply of milk to those mothers who have twins. One doctor insisted that his patient nurse her twin babies because he felt it would be easier for her. It is the only way a mother can feed two babies at the same time!

In addition, a few mothers with one breast have been encouraged by their doctors to nurse in order to reduce the chance of developing cancer in the remaining breast. The American Cancer Society and the National Cancer Institute of the USPH Service report that cancer of the breast is more apt to develop in those breasts that do not give milk, and scientific studies confirm the fact that *long-term* nursing lowers the breast-cancer risk.

These examples are given to show you, not only how lactation can be encouraged under unusual or different circumstances, but above all to impress upon you, as a mother, that you certainly can nurse your baby under normal conditions. The important thing to remember is that breast-feeding can be a very easy and natural affair. God gave you your baby and He also provided you with

1. Jennie Buckner and Jocelyn Kreiger, "She's Breastfeeding Her Adopted Baby," *Detroit Free Press*, August 27, 1972.

the best food for your baby, food that you alone can give him. To help you feed your baby, He gave your infant a strong urge to suck. It's that simple. Let the baby suck often at the breast and you will have plenty of milk for his nourishment.

THE BREAST AS A PACIFIER

This brings us to another important point. Babies have an obvious need to suck. They will suck on anything they come in contact with—breast, fingers, clothing, or objects. This is a normal, healthy habit that should be encouraged (the baby or older child will outgrow it easily later if his desire to suck isn't frustrated early in life), and one that is particularly well satisfied at the mother's breast.

The breast is nature's pacifier for the baby. This is hard for many mothers to appreciate in our culture, where breast-feeding is unpopular and where the artificial feeding of infants is the preferred practice. We tend to forget that these artificial aids— bottles and pacifiers—are merely substitutes for mother. The infant's need to suck or to be pacified at the breast is nature's way of bringing mother and baby together at other than feeding times.

The breast produces the same effect as a bottle or a soother—that is, it calms the infant, which is often the way the baby likes to feel before going to sleep. The breast-fed baby wants the breast for this "pacifying" need of his just as another baby prefers his bottle or soother. This is why the nursing mother cannot really say how many times she has fed the baby during the day. Does she count the times she has pacified her baby into a deep sleep —even though her baby might have acquired little milk in the process? The breast also offers security and

4

comfort. It brings love and reassurance any time during the day or night.

Sucking is also apparently a very satisfying experience in itself. Dr. James Hymes, author of *The Child Under Six*,[2] says that sucking provides babies with many pleasant sensations, and in *The First Nine Months*[3] Geraldine Lux Flanagan points out that some babies are born with a callus on their thumb as a result of their sucking activity in the womb. Surely this is an indication that sucking was a satisfying experience for these babies even before birth.

Perhaps this is a good place to begin to explain what is meant by the subtitle of this book, "The Ecology of Natural Mothering." Strictly speaking, ecology is concerned with the relationship between living things and their environment. Frequently it is a rather delicate relationship, and every week we read about how this or that animal or fish or tree may be affected by such and such a change in the environment. The language of ecology is applied less frequently to human relationships, but it is still valid. For example, there is a gentle, ecological relationship between the breast-feeding baby and his mother. The more he sucks, the more milk she has for him.

Another aspect of this breast-feeding ecology is the relationship between the emotional and physiological needs of the infant. Both needs are satisfied through sucking at the breast. The hungry baby gets not only nutrition but also emotional satisfaction through the sucking and through being picked up and held. The baby who sucks primarily for some emotional satisfaction also gets some nourishment and by his sucking helps reinforce his mother's milk supply. The mother can continue to satisfy the emotional need at the breast even when her baby has a nutritional need for other foods in addition to breast milk. This helps to explain why some cultures that are sensitive to the child's needs think nothing of continuing some breast-feeding even into the third and fourth years.

The frequent stimulation of the breast by the baby also plays an important role in maintaining natural infertility after childbirth. This and other aspects of the breast-feeding ecology will be spelled out in later chapters. Suffice it to say for now that Mother Nature

2. Englewood Cliffs: Prentice-Hall, 1963.
3. New York: Pocket Books, 1962.

has provided a mutually beneficial relationship in breast-feeding and provides many opportunities for its proper development.

SUCKING STIMULUS AND OVULATION

When a young girl reaches puberty, she normally begins to experience the menstrual cycle. If she has prepared for this as a natural development, she accepts it as part of becoming an adult woman and may give it little further thought. On the other hand, she may have wanted a better understanding of her bodily functions and sought out the whole story behind her monthly cycle. If you are such a woman, the following facts will scarcely be new; but certain facts take on new relevance when seen in relation to child-bearing and child spacing.

At puberty the two ovaries within the female body become active. At this time the eggs inside the ovary begin to mature, and each egg or ovum during its development becomes encased in a sac of fluid called a *follicle*. As the eggs or ova develop, one ovum at a time migrates, or approaches the surface of the ovary. At the surface the follicle ruptures, releasing the ovum. The ovum is now free to travel from the ovary down the Fallopian tubes toward the womb or uterus. This process of the release of the ovum is necessary before fertilization or conception takes place, and is called *ovulation*.

While the body is preparing for ovulation, the lining of the uterus is thickening to receive the ovum should conception occur. If the ovum is not fertilized, the lining of the uterus is sloughed off and bleeding occurs. This bleeding is known as *menstruation* or *menses*. It is often referred to as a "menstrual period" or "menstrual cycle."

If pregnancy occurs, however, a change occurs in the body chemistry. One effect of this is that the lining of the womb is not sloughed off but remains built up, thereby eliminating menstrual bleeding during the pregnancy. This is termed *pregnancy amenorrhea*. Amenorrhea simply means "not having periods." Another effect of this change in the body chemistry during pregnancy is that the ovaries remain at rest; no ovulation and no additional pregnancy can occur until after childbirth. The only exception would be multiple conceptions, but it is known that when double or triple ovulations occur in a cycle they all occur within the same twenty-four-hour period.

Our interest in this whole process is the continuation of this infertile condition following childbirth. If the mother nurses her baby properly, she will normally retain this infertile condition by experiencing a lengthy absence from menstrual periods following birth. This is known as *lactation amenorrhea*. The medical researchers have been unable to describe with certainty the body chemistry involved, but there seems to be fairly general agreement that the sucking stimulus by the infant at the breast is responsible for the body chemistry that provides this natural infertility.

It is also apparent that the amount and frequency of sucking is very closely related to the natural infertility of breast-feeding. Therefore, there are two practical conclusions for the nursing mother who would like this side benefit of breast-feeding. First of all, she should positively cooperate with her baby's natural desires to suckle whether it be for nutritional or emotional needs. Secondly, she should avoid those practices that prematurely lessen her baby's feeding at the breast. This would include almost the entire range of cultural baby-care practices in the United States: early solids and liquids other than mother's milk, rigid nursing schedules, pacifiers, the race to get baby sleeping through the night, baby-sitters, and so on.

The guidelines that are given in this book go hand in hand with what I call "natural mothering." By natural mothering I mean that care of an infant in which his needs are met primarily by the mother, and not by artifacts or baby-sitters. It is natural baby care as well, for the mother follows her baby's natural development or pattern. Natural mothering, then, is not ruled by clocks or schedules; instead, the baby is the mother's guide.

It is one thing to state the guidelines for natural spacing; it is something else to put a natural mothering program into practice in the face of some current customs of child care. Unfortunately, many of the current practices today restrict or eliminate the mothering that nature intended, and seriously interfere with the natural infertility of breast-feeding. Because these factors take the baby away from his mother, the following chapters will look at these cultural practices in more detail, to see how they hinder nature's plan for spacing babies.

2

Does Complete Mean Total?

In the last chapter the infertility of pregnancy was compared with the infertility of breast-feeding, and the absence of ovulation and menstruation was noted in both. One thing that is evident is that the developing baby in the mother's womb derives 100 percent of its nourishment from its mother. The point that cannot be over-stressed with regard to breast-feeding and ovulation is that the baby who gives his mother the natural infertility of breast-feeding will also be getting 100 percent of his nourishment from his mother's breast. Less than 100 percent is weaning,[1] and nowhere do I want to give the impression that early weaning guarantees the same degree of infertility as complete or total breast-feeding does.

In a society conditioned to look to the doctor for assistance in every phase of life, and especially in the areas of infant nutrition, it is difficult to be understood when speaking about complete breast-feeding. Complete breast-feeding doesn't require any for-mulas, any juice, any baby foods, or any special concoctions. (I

1. Weaning refers to the process of introducing a breast-fed baby to other foods or liquids. This process can last two days, two weeks, twelve months, or three years. It begins as soon as the mother offers her baby something else for nourishment besides breast milk; it ends the day that her baby no longer takes any milk from the breast. From this definition, it can be said that many mothers wean their babies from the day they leave the hospital, even though they actually nurse for six or ten months. In addition, the baby also undergoes an emotional weaning off the breast, gradually receiving this emotional nourishment from other sources and contacts and from his mother in other ways.

am not considering the case of the sick baby who may need special treatment. I am speaking only about the normal healthy baby.) However, the fact is that in recent years most doctors have prescribed formulas and set up definite schedules for the introduction of juices, liquids, cereals, and solids. Most mothers have thus come to believe that this was medically, nutritionally, and psychologically the "best" way, and breast-feeding is either looked down upon as fit for only the lower social groups or as a nice but very short-run supplement to the "real" nourishment put out by the food and drug companies. I'll have more to say about the role of the doctor in the life of the breast-feeding couple later; my present purpose is to illustrate the difficulty of being correctly understood in the context of contemporary practice.

Complete or total breast-feeding means, again, that the baby derives all his food from his mother's breasts. It means that the only nipples that need to be in the house are part of the mother's natural equipment. It should go without saying that there does not have to be a baby bottle in the house.

Now I have nothing against the mother who bottle-feeds or who partially breast-feeds. My only complaint comes when the mother who partially breast-feeds tells her friends that she is nursing and that, of course, her menstrual periods have started or that she became pregnant. I want to agree with the "of course," but I also want to make it clear that her partial breast-feeding is what I call weaning, not total or complete breast-feeding.

If I seem somewhat repetitious on this point, it's because I am convinced that misunderstanding is so widespread that a single statement is not sufficient. Perhaps the following examples will illustrate why I think the idea needs clarification.

In 1967 a mother wrote to *Our Sunday Visitor* saying that if breast-feeding "is done properly it will suspend ovulation and menstruation for seven to fifteen months." She encouraged other mothers to give it a try, as "it is still God's plan for spacing babies." Some letters were printed several weeks later showing the various responses to her letter. The following are excerpts from some of those letters.

I know a mother who had nine children in eleven years; she breast-fed each until a new pregnancy forced her to stop. . . .

I also have a friend who is a nurse and breast-feeds every baby and in six years has had four babies and two miscarriages. . . .

I think probably a mother who nurses during the first three months would suppress ovulation but not for seven to fifteen months . . . and then only if it is complete nursing with no supplement foods and most doctors would want you to start other foods at least by three months.

A close friend sent me the newspaper clippings of these letters with a note attached: "I think that these ladies who object to nursing as a natural baby spacer probably don't know enough about it. I mean about *no* solids or supplements."

One time after I had just finished explaining total breast-feeding to a mother she said, "Well, that can't be true. I nursed and still had my periods." After a few questions were asked of her, she said: "Oh, yes. I gave a bottle to my babies."

Another mother gave a similar response after being told about the spacing benefit of breast-feeding. "Well, I nursed my babies for ten months and always had periods." She was asked if she gave the baby anything else. "Oh, yes," she said. "You don't expect a baby to get along on just breast milk, do you?"

And a mother who expressed an interest in natural child spacing referred to herself, after some discussion, as "only nursing"; yet earlier in the conversation she had mentioned giving her baby several bottles of juice during the day to keep the baby on a four-hour schedule.

Mothers who do become interested in natural child spacing eventually find themselves talking about this aspect of breast-feeding with their friends and relatives. Most of their acquaintances will admit that they do not remember when they introduced solids or the bottle when they nursed their babies nor do they remember when their periods returned. Some mothers, however, do insist that they became pregnant while nursing, but usually later conversations bring out the fact that they were weaning at the time of conception. One mother insisted on several different occasions that she became pregnant while only nursing her baby, but later talked about how she gave solids to her babies at three months. As her relative told her, "There you go. There's your answer. You weren't completely nursing." Another mother insisted likewise, but it was later learned that she gave supplementary feedings a few weeks after the birth of her babies. A third mother who was sure that she became pregnant while completely nursing later said that she was giving her baby "only juice at the time." These actual remarks convince me that many people do not understand what is meant by complete or total breast-feeding.

I consider myself more fortunate than many. With our first child the obstetrician discouraged me with regard to breast-feeding, and especially with regard to its natural effect of spacing babies. He was very firm and negative on this point, and I accepted his views. However, with our second child I had a different obstetrician, who listened to my desire to nurse the baby and to my questions about child spacing through breast-feeding. He affirmed the spacing effect, but only if I nursed totally. He told me to use nothing but breast milk to nourish the baby. I remember asking him, "What about water?" And he answered, "Not even water." I was told to nurse my baby in this manner for as long as I desired—and I found this most welcome advice.

The truth of the matter is that when a mother provides (1) all of her baby's nourishment at her breast and (2) the greater part of his other sucking needs at her breast, she will almost invariably experience the side effect of natural infertility. You can have child spacing (using other means) without breast-feeding, but you cannot normally have breast-feeding in the sense described above without the side effect of child spacing. To put it another way, if a woman should sincerely want to become pregnant within six months following childbirth, she should not follow the breast-feeding plan described in this chapter.

I want to call special attention to the second part of the statement above in boldface type, "the greater part of his other sucking needs." Some mothers have been very disappointed to experience menstruation or conception while totally breast-feeding. Too often, however, these mothers are restricting the nursing by not following the other aspects of natural mothering. In other words, the total breast-feeding rule is no guarantee that menstruation or ovulation will not occur. A mother who follows the total breast-feeding *nutrition* rule may not be satisfying her child's other needs at the breast. May I give you a true example?

A breast-feeding mother phoned for information on natural family planning—information neither the hospital nor her doctor could give her. Knowing that she had nursed her babies, we discussed natural spacing. She wasn't initially interested in reading the material I had gathered on the subject, but I encouraged her to do so to see if she really was an exception—for she was convinced that she was the odd case. She had totally breast-fed all her babies, yet experienced regular menstrual periods three and one-half to four weeks after childbirth with all six children. She never once experienced an absence of periods while nursing. In addition, she was nursing her sixth baby often, day and night. Upon returning the material, she wrote:

First, an apology—someone had told me that you were "far-out" and I accepted the opinion without investigation. Our problem in nursing probably lies in not letting Jane suck long enough. I usually have a fast flow. She is satisfied in about eight to ten minutes. I also have used both breasts to fill her up to save time. She sucks her finger, and this indicates a need for more sucking. I do nurse lying down as often as possible, but I've seldom let the baby fall asleep with me. I feel that my practice of nursing quickly also is at fault. Don't you? Let me try some of your suggestions and we'll see what happens.

The suggestions the mother was referring to were those in the material I had given her, as normally I do not suggest a change in nursing or mothering habits for those interested in natural family planning *if* menstruation has already occurred.

About six months later I happened to meet this mother, and learned from her that she experienced lactation amenorrhea for the first time. Her baby was four months old when her periods stopped and she went four months without menstrual bleeding. This particular case illustrates that there is much more to natural spacing than merely filling baby's tummy or satisfying hunger pangs by total breast-feeding.

In the past the total breast-feeding nutrition rule has been the only guideline taught to mothers who were interested in nursing and in avoiding an immediate pregnancy. True, that rule is extremely important, but it's only one aspect of the overall natural-spacing picture. Other guidelines are also important, and deserve as much attention and emphasis.

3

New Light on Night Feedings

This topic does not appeal to many mothers, but it may be an important one to consider if you are interested in natural child spacing. Night feedings are frequently normal for a breast-fed baby. Many infants need one night feeding—and oftentimes several—during the first or even the second year of life. These feedings are important for several reasons, the most obvious being that they form a part of the baby's nutrition. In line with that, it should be noted that the regularity of the sucking tends to produce a regular supply of milk. From the point of view of natural child spacing, night feedings are important because the same sucking stimulus that brings on an ample supply of milk also affects the body chemistry that is responsible for the natural-spacing mechanism. A mother who anticipated that her breast-feeding would result in both a healthy baby and natural infertility would hardly go for ten or twelve hours without nursing during the day. She should likewise not set a goal of so many hours without nursing her baby during the night. The absence of any feedings for any length of time may initiate an early return of one's menstrual periods, and thereby shorten the time during which a mother is unable to conceive while nursing. If you want the natural child-spacing effect of breast-feeding, then give your baby the night feedings he will naturally desire.

NIGHT FEEDINGS AND CONTEMPORARY
SOCIAL ATTITUDES

Many modern parents might concede the biological necessity of night feedings to provide the body chemistry balance for natural infertility, but at the same time they might find themselves muttering that night feedings don't seem so very natural. In fact, they seem directly contrary to "doing what comes natcherly." Here we run into the conflict between contemporary social attitudes and a more natural process.

Contemporary emphasis is placed on getting the baby to sleep all the way through the night and at the earliest possible date. The longer the baby sleeps at night, the better he is thought to be. Parents pride themselves on the speed with which they can get their new baby to sleep the entire night. They learn to stuff the baby before bedtime with the hope that this will satisfy him for the duration of the night. If the baby does wake, they hope that the fussing or crying will only be temporary, so that they will not have to get out of bed—for which no one can blame them. When those hopes fail and they have to get up, they might have to go to the bother of warming up a bottle; and by the time that chore is done—to the tune of the baby's continued crying—all they are hoping for is that the baby will feed himself back to sleep without further ado. But then there's the problem of the air that the baby took in from the bottle. Now he needs burping, and that means a second trip from the bed to baby. With this type of routine it's no wonder that bottle-feeding parents aim for that goal of "all through the night as early as possible."

Others hope to do the trick with the pacifier. As one mother put it rather bluntly, "Let's face it. We stick the pacifier back in their mouths, hoping they'll settle down and go back to sleep again." Another answer to the problem was recommended recently by a doctor to a friend of mine. He told the couple to put the baby in the bathroom, close the door, and let the baby cry it out.

The breast-feeding mother is likewise warned not to fall asleep while nursing or she will crush or smother her child. Thus, getting up to feed her baby becomes a tiresome chore, and she soon longs for a full night's rest. Books on child care and breast-feeding usually discourage night feedings for the older baby; the general advice is that the two-to-five-month-old baby doesn't need them anyway. So the nursing mother is instructed to wean the baby from night feedings at a very early age. If the baby objects, she is sometimes advised to ignore his cries and stuff cotton in her ears.[1] She may be told to offer him a bottle or to let her husband take care of the baby because all the baby wants is his mother anyway! One mother we know was recently advised by her doctor to give her two-month-old baby a drug so it would sleep through the night. Fortunately, or unfortunately, most babies sleep away from their mothers anyway, and soon begin to learn to sleep through the night on their own. They never have the pleasure of receiving from their mother during the night hours that touch stimulation said to be so important.

The problem of night feeding, however, is partially eliminated by a change of attitudes, by simply looking to the best interests of the baby instead of to our own convenience. During my first three years of mothering, I happened to have frequent contact with a small group of women who placed a great deal of emphasis on the needs of their babies. Good mothering meant meeting baby's needs during the night as well as during the day. Therefore, it was common to hear a mother speak of night feedings when her child was twelve months old or even eighteen months old. When we moved, I soon learned that such a group was in the minority, that most people have entirely different views about raising children compared to those views I had acquired from my original exposure. In our new environment, it seemed that the question most frequently asked about our baby was: "Is she sleeping through the night now?" or "How often do you have to feed her during the night?" According to this viewpoint, night feedings are a problem to be conquered instead of simply part of the process of child care.

The answer to such questions is rather simple. Our children will never take a prize for all-night sleeping at an early age. My husband and I learned that this is one phase they outgrow when

1. Alice Gerard, *Please Breastfeed Your Baby* (New York: New American Library, 1970), p. 97.

they are ready; and not only are there many advantages to both parent and baby in letting nature take its course in this area, but doing so eliminates all the worries and problems inherent in training a child to sleep through the night.

Our first two children awoke for night feedings every night until we decided that it might be time to stop this "habit." When they were both eighteen months old, we tried all the tricks and none worked. So we resorted to the "crying it out" scheme. That worked within two or three nights. We would never do it this way again if we had another chance, but at that time we were uninformed. We didn't really feel this was the best way, but we conformed to our society's norms and thus made our children also conform.

With our third child, we promised ourselves that she would have the freedom to grow in every area at her pace. Well past her third birthday she was still crawling into bed with us at some time during the wee hours for some nursing. I must admit that there were a few times when she was two years old that we almost weakened. However, at these times support came in one form or another.

Some of this support came in the form of writings, to which I will refer later. Other support came through personal acquaintances and correspondence. I learned from a friend that her child, although weaned when ten months old, didn't sleep naturally through the night until she was four and a half years old. And in talking with mothers, I learned that many have a similar situation at night, regardless of whether they chose to bottle-feed or breast-feed. However, since babies are "supposed" to sleep through the night, many mothers do not admit it or like to talk about it. Likewise, I was fortunate to be able to correspond with other nursing mothers, and found that there was always someone else who was night-nursing a baby older than ours. You can't imagine how much support this was!

We are pleased with the results. In our experience, taking care of the child's real needs at this early stage does not set a pattern for the development of an emotionally unstable child who is filled with all sorts of imagined needs later on. Quite the opposite. Nor does the child who grows out of night feedings at his own pace never outgrow them. Our child who was still coming in during the night at three and a half, was, at four and a half, not only sleeping all through the night but was the last one to wake up in the morning.

HOW TO FEED YOUR BABY AT NIGHT

Nighttime feedings are no bother when mothers generally nurse in bed and fall asleep while doing so. "Horrors! What kind of a mother would admit to falling asleep while nursing her baby in bed? Doesn't she realize that many mothers smother their babies in bed?" These are common fears expressed by doctors, nurses, and acquaintances. These are fears that I also had with our first child. I heard about the advantages of nursing in bed, but I still couldn't overcome my fears of giving it a try, and would sit in a chair for the night feedings. Oftentimes I was cold, and I was always tired. After fifteen or twenty minutes of breast-feeding, I would take the baby off the breast even though she wanted to suck more in her sleep.

With our next baby, a nursing mother encouraged me to try nursing the baby in bed. This time I was open to the idea, tried it, and found that it made all the difference in the world. It became a convenience instead of an inconvenience, and it required only the time it took to bring the baby to bed or to roll over and offer the breast if she was already there.

I find that other nursing mothers are also reluctant to give it a try. They have these same acquired fears. Eventually some of them do give it a try, and then they begin to rave about the advantages of lying down to nurse the baby.

The fact that there is a natural maternal instinct to protect one's baby cannot be ignored; indeed, it is a good thing. Certainly, you must make sure your blankets or pillows are not near his face, or that your husband will not pull the blankets up over the baby. The baby may be dressed in a warm trundle bundle so that he may lie on top of the blankets. Other mothers tuck the baby right under the blankets, knowing he will turn his head completely away from the breast or up toward the head of the bed. Some mothers nurse with the baby in the center of the bed so that he will not fall off the bed, and they learn to offer the baby both breasts without switching him to the other side.

If the father is a light sleeper, the baby can sleep on the other side of his mother, near the side of the bed. When the baby is small, a hamper or chair can be placed at the side of the bed to prevent him from falling. Having a big, roomy bed, such as a king-size, is an asset to this type of program, although I have known parents who slept with their child in a regular double bed. Other arrangements have also been made. Some couples have slept on mattresses right on the floor, with the child's mattress right next to theirs. The child can be nursed and then returned to his own mattress.

This same arrangement has been done with beds. The child's bed is placed next to the parents' bed, on his mother's side. This close arrangement still allows the mother to nurse without restrictions: the child can be nursed as long as desired and still receive much cuddling in the process. The mother then has the option of returning the child to his bed later.

Some mothers find it difficult to nurse lying down at first, and some are never comfortable in any lying-down position. One mother who could not nurse lying down used a comfortable lounging chair for night feedings. Whichever way you choose, the important thing during the night is to be physically close enough to your child to sense his needs and to allow the child to nurse at his leisure without your getting tired.

Needless to say, if a mother has been drinking or has been taking sleeping pills or is incapacitated in some way, it would not be a good practice to take the baby to bed with her that night. However, the point I would like to make is that the experience of nursing mothers shows that the baby who nurses in his mother's bed runs no more risk of being smothered than he would with a bottle and blanket in his own crib.

One of the most reliable and authoritative sources on the subject of breast-feeding is La Leche League International. Literally thousands of mothers have relied on its advice and guidance, and as a result have found that nursing in bed is a very safe practice. One friend wrote of her original fears about nursing her baby in bed and then of her subsequent relief.

When I had my first baby, I was warned again and again not to nurse her in bed because I might fall asleep and she might smother. But I wound up doing it anyhow. Sometimes I fell asleep and then felt terribly guilty. It wasn't until LLL and my number-five baby that I put aside all such fears and just relaxed.

Hoping that I have quieted some opposition on this point, I'd like to point out what I believe are some definite advantages to nighttime feedings, some of which are related to nursing in bed.

THE ADVANTAGES OF NIGHT FEEDINGS

It has already been said that the nursing mother finds that she can satisfy her child's needs with little inconvenience or loss of sleep. Being so close to her child, the mother can wake up temporarily at his first stir to offer him the breast. The child does not have to stir and stir and then finally cry to get her attention as he would if he were in a separate room. After offering the breast, the mother then dozes back to sleep. This becomes so easy and natural that often she could not say, if asked, how many times she nursed during the night. Nursing a baby is one job she can do well in her sleep.

A well-known advantage of breast-feeding is that the convenience eliminates a lot of decision making, and possibly arguing, between husband and wife. They do not have to decide who shall take care of the baby when it stirs or who will get up to warm the bottle. If the baby is already in their bed or next to it, the husband has another advantage—he doesn't have to get up even to bring the baby to bed.

Still another advantage is the restfulness a mother can derive from nursing in bed or lying down for naps. In fact, mothers who claim to be the nervous type have noted the tranquilizing effect of breast-feeding. Nursing can be a quieting and peaceful respite in the midst of noise, anxieties, and irritations. This is why some mothers will pick up their babies and nurse them on the rare night that they cannot sleep. Nursing, besides putting baby to sleep, can also put the mother to sleep. In addition, no matter how often or how long the baby nurses during the night, the mother is well rested generally, and this restfulness is truly a big bonus for the entire family. Mother can function better and enjoy her family; her good disposition makes for a smoothly running day. She, likewise, is not resentful—the baby did not keep her up all night, nor did her husband sleep through the night while she was up with the baby. Indeed, the practice of night feedings as recommended in this book may well improve family living.

What about burping? Do you have to get up to burp your baby? Very frequently the baby who requires an occasional burping during the day will not require any burping at night. For a newborn who does require burping, it is easy to place his head and shoulder area up over your hip or stomach as you lie in bed.

Mothers have also written about how much they enjoyed these nightly snuggles with their baby. The cuddly, close relationship seems to have an emotional charge for the mother. But what's in it for father? Again, it comes down to a question of attitudes. Properly informed, he can see the advantages for the child, his wife, and himself. One friend who was excited about his wife's pregnancy said, "Boy, I think it's going to be great to have the baby sleeping with us." Fathers have found that they enjoy this "bedtime" closeness, that they like waking up with their child at their side. Some parents readily ask whether this practice will interfere with the intimacy between husband and wife. Certainly there are alternatives. At times of intimacy it is hardly necessary to bring the baby to bed until afterwards, when you are ready to sleep. A couple who know their baby will awake

soon may not choose to bring the baby to bed until later. Likewise, marital intimacies do not have to be confined to the bedroom.

Breast-feeding in bed has advantages for the baby, too. This is one time when he can suck to full contentment in quiet, cozy surroundings. This is a time when his mother won't be interrupted, a time when he can use the breast as a pacifier to fulfill his sucking needs. It is known that babies at times will nurse on and off for several hours while mother sleeps. This is common in the older breast-fed child as well.

The most striking advantage is that this practice seems to play an important role in the child's emotional development because the baby keeps in *touch* with mother. The baby has a critical need for bodily contact with his mother; he *needs* to be caressed, cuddled, held, or just to be carried about with his mother. Some psychologists and writers today are quite concerned that most babies receive very little contact with their mother. This physical closeness with mother is all too often lacking, especially in our American culture.

An excellent article, "Of Babies, Beds and Teddy Bears" by Kenny and Schreiter,[2] documents the need for the infant to be in physical touch with his mother. Sleeping with one's baby is strongly encouraged, and support for this practice is given from psychological studies of other cultures. They show how sleeping together was once an American tradition until twin beds became so popular in recent history. Good mothering is defined as much holding and cuddling of the baby, with emphasis given to sleeping together at night. Readers may study this article in its entire form in the Appendix section of this book.

Ashley Montagu, in his book *Touching: The Human Significance of the Skin,*[3] demonstrates that the skin is the most important sensory organ we have and that the child needs to receive much skin stimulation from its mother in order to survive physically and emotionally. The sense of touch on the skin is the most alert sense during sleep, and therefore sleeping with babies is recommended. He uses other cultures as an example of that type of "touch" mothering which is so lacking in the American mother. Sleeping

2. *Marriage,* January 1971.
3. New York: Columbia University Press, 1971.

with the child is characteristic of the mother in these cultures where the child has lots of skin-to-skin contact with mother and, of course, where breast-feeding is common.

One of the most noted researchers in the area of mothering and lactation is Niles Newton. In recent articles and speeches she has depicted the differences between bottle-feeding, token breast-feeding, and unrestricted breast-feeding. Token breast-feeding is typical of the American nursing mother today. Nursing is very limited; the baby receives little contact with mother; the baby sleeps in a different room because sleeping with the baby is considered dangerous; weaning occurs within a few weeks. However, with unrestricted breast-feeding, nursing is not restricted by rules; the child sleeps with or near his mother; the child has easy access to the breast day and night; no bottles are given to the baby and solids are begun only when baby is ready; the weaning process continues into early childhood. In addition, she notes that another characteristic of unrestricted nursing is a lengthy absence from menstrual periods.[4] Newton's description of unrestricted breast-feeding is exactly the type of mothering program I find necessary for natural spacing.

The mother who follows this pattern of unrestricted nursing experiences another aspect of the ecology of natural mothering. By taking care of the baby's needs for closeness, cuddling, and skin contact during the night, she also provides the opportunity for her baby to nurse as often as he pleases. The usual side effect of this, of course, is that his sucking helps prolong the period of natural infertility. But I think it is important for a mother to do things for the right reasons, so I don't recommend night feedings or other aspects of natural mothering *just* to prolong amenorrhea. They should come out of the mother's realization that the nighttime closeness and nursing are good for both the baby and herself, and that the extended amenorrhea is just a natural side effect.

If this approach were taken generally, then there would be fewer mothers who complain that to experience breast-feeding's natural infertility they would have to set the alarm, get up a couple times during the night to get the baby, and so on. I sympathize with these mothers because they have knowingly or unknowingly

4. Niles Newton, "Battle Between Breast and Bottle," *Psychology Today*, July 1972, p. 70.

adopted the practices of a Western culture that goes strongly against the natural practices of unrestricted nursing. It is difficult to achieve the natural side effects of breast-feeding when part of the natural relationship is thwarted. Perhaps the question these mothers —and dads, too—should ask is, "If I were the baby, wouldn't I rather be close to my mommy instead of all by myself? If I woke up during the night, wouldn't I rather be next to nice warm Mommy who is ready to feed me rather than in a room with nobody else around?"

Yes, there are those who recommend the "tough" approach. "Make the baby realize that life is tough all over. Introduce it to the 'real world' as soon as possible." I disagree, and not only because the tough approach restricts the nursing pattern. It also incorporates a view of life that is very incomplete. In the real world, we soon realize that we can't make it on our own; we need a friend, someone who will bear with us even when we are less than perfect. So why not begin from the earliest months to let the baby know the friendship of his mother?

From everything said thus far, it should be evident that the mother who adopts this natural mothering approach isn't going to be thinking in terms of getting her baby to sleep through the night. She will let the baby set the pace. In fact, if the baby is an unusually heavy sleeper, she will want to encourage—not force— a nursing when she goes to bed and again when she first awakens. This relieves her breasts of excessive fullness and helps maintain a steady milk supply. It is also, according to some mothers, a most pleasant experience to nurse a sleepy baby at these times. The breast fullness seems to be nature's way of reminding the mother of her baby—and to be near her baby. It also helps the baby to get a regular intake of nourishment.

In summary, if a baby wakes up at night because of a need that can be fulfilled at the breast, there is no easier and better way for the family to get back to sleep than by letting the baby nurse at his mother's side in bed. This not only helps to satisfy the baby's nutritional and emotional needs, but satisfies the emotional needs of the mother: not only in that it is restful for her, but she derives satisfaction in doing what is best for her baby and from having a contented and quiet baby as a result.

Sleeping with baby is an important practice for a mother to consider if she desires to space babies naturally—especially in our culture, where it is the custom to encourage babies to sleep through the night and to sleep apart from mother. These feedings help to maintain a more regular periodic feeding pattern throughout the twenty-four-hour day. They thus continue to provide frequent stimulation to the mother's breast and subsequently influence her body chemistry toward natural infertility.

4

Pacification of the Baby

Pacifiers have strongly influenced mothering today. They are of special interest here, since they limit the amount of sucking and mothering at the breast. In fact, when regularly offered, the pacifier often receives more attention from the baby than the bottle or the breast.

We have already spoken of the role that the breast plays in pacifying the baby. It is also true that not only the breast but the mother's entire body plays an important role here as well. Her body is very adaptable. Her fingers can stroke and tease. When the baby is too little to put his hand up to his mouth, her own knuckle or chin can act as a "pacifier" when the baby does not desire the breast. Her face offers expressions of love and happiness that tell the baby that he is someone very special. Her body offers motion and rhythm—two things babies love, and which they receive when their mothers hold them, rock them, or carry them. The mother provides an "infant seat" for her baby when she sits and crosses one knee. Certain leg positions can form a cradle for her baby; when her legs move, baby is gently rocked. A good mother is needed, and no one can replace her. Sometimes her presence is all that is needed to change a baby's cries into smiles. Truly, a mother is the best pacifier for her baby.

I have been told that in former generations, when breast-feeding was commonplace, some nursing mothers used various objects that served the same purposes as our rubber pacifiers. However, the present enormous popularity of the nipple-shaped pacifier seems to have started in the early 1950s. If this is correct, it more or less coincides with the large American family of those days when mothers were sometimes having babies every year and were almost exclusively bottle-feeding and using the products of the baby foods industry. In the absence of breast-feeding, it is small wonder why those mothers flocked to the pacifier for their babies.

WHY A PACIFIER?

The most obvious reason for offering the pacifier is to soothe and comfort the baby without nursing. Less obviously, it is also used to pacify the parent, who is thus spared the trouble of nursing or just holding the baby; parents tend to put the baby whose cries have been silenced by the pacifier back into the infant seat, crib, or playpen as soon as they can get away with doing so.

Some nursing mothers claim that they can't get along without the pacifier. Their baby is too fussy or they have too much milk and the baby wants to suck on an empty breast, not a full one. Let's take a look at these reasons.

"The Baby Is Too Fussy"

It can be expected that most babies will have an occasional fussy spell. This doesn't mean that it will happen every day, but it may happen several times during the week. Some mothers may find that it seems a common occurrence in the early evening hours or when a baby is teething. It is always helpful to remember that eventually the baby will outgrow this fussiness. In addition, some babies will be alert and awake for a long period of time although they will not be fussy in an uncomfortable sense. Instead, they want lots of cuddling and holding or the presence of their mothers. Fortunately, there are other ways to soothe a baby without resorting to the pacifier. After all, women got along without them for years!

Here are some suggestions:

1. Make sure the baby is neither too cold nor too warm; many mothers tend to overdress a baby.

2. Offer the breast, or see first if baby is interested by placing him in the nursing position.

3. Rock, hold, carry, walk, sway, dance, or sing to the baby. Rub or pat his back. Try lying down on your back and placing the baby on top of you; the movements of your chest may comfort him. A husband can be a big help here when nursing isn't the answer.

4. Take a warm bath with the baby. Babies love to take baths with their mothers or bigger brothers and sisters. There's more physical contact and security for the baby, it's easier and more fun for mother, and it has a relaxing effect on both. You may find that afterwards the baby will nurse into a deep sleep.

5. Weather permitting, take baby for a walk outdoors. Baby slings and back carriers are ideal for this type of activity. Some babies nurse and sleep well in the car, so, if it's a weekend, maybe you and your husband would like to take a drive out in the country.

6. Offer the breast again. A baby may refuse the breast initially and yet welcome it only fifteen minutes later.

7. Let the baby use natural pacifiers at times he is not interested in the breast—his fingers, your chin, and so on.

There may be a time when none of the above suggestions will help. I have had friends who had colicky babies, and they have remarked that the best thing to do was just continue the 100 percent nursing and give them lots of the physical contact all babies need. The husband's help and support during this time was especially important to them. With most babies, however, the fussiness is brief, and normally a mother can find a more "natural" solution to baby's discomfort than using a pacifier.

"I Have Too Much Milk"

There will be times for most babies when it looks as if they are having difficulty handling the milk that comes from their mother's breast. The milk comes too fast and the baby is inclined to fuss and pull away from the breast temporarily until the milk flow slows down. It is a situation more common for the baby in his early months; as he grows older, he will enjoy this ample supply. Other babies have satisfied their need for food but desire to suck more. What they want is an empty breast, not one full of milk; so they react quite strongly against the breast that is full.

There really isn't any problem in the first situation. The occasional time that this happens the mother can allow for more burping or wait until the "let-down" feeling—which is what causes the milk to come out so fast—has been completed. But don't wait if baby is crying, please. If baby is hungry, he'll be anxious to get back on the breast. So let him; if it's too much for him to handle again, he'll pull off and keep trying. If, however, this situation occurs at almost every feeding, you might find some of these ideas helpful:

1. Try a different nursing position, such as lying down. At night mothers seldom have this problem when sleeping with the baby.

2. Try offering the breast so that the spray angles off to the side or top of the baby's mouth and not directly toward the back of his throat.

3. Offer one breast only at a feeding. This way the baby can satisfy his other sucking needs toward the end of the feeding on a breast that isn't full of milk. A small infant can receive plenty of milk from one breast at a feeding, especially when the supply is ample. At the next feeding offer the other breast.

4. The mother who has a huge supply for a month or two after childbirth might offer the same breast for approximately a three-hour period. In other words, she would feed the baby, let's say, at 9:00 A.M. Then, if an hour later the baby wanted to nurse again, the mother would offer the same breast she offered at 9:00, and so on up until noon. During the next two- to three-hour period she would offer the other breast. This feeding pattern could be used until the milk supply settled and the baby could handle it better.

Normally, one-breast feedings with unrestricted nursing do not present any problems. However, since in using this method there is an increased risk of engorgement or a plugged duct with an abundant supply of milk, the mother should be observant. If a breast becomes too full and drippy, she can express the excess milk.[1] If a tender spot is felt on the breast, she can let the baby suck on that breast as much as possible to keep it empty (plus additional hand expression during a let-down, if necessary), and usually the tenderness will disappear as quickly as it appeared.

Proper management of an overabundant milk supply may be a factor in the maintenance of infertility. For example, one mother

1. For instructions on how to express milk, see the La Leche League manual, *The Womanly Art of Breastfeeding* (Franklin Park, Ill.).

wrote that she had so much milk that her four-month-old was not sucking for the milk. She said her milk supply was so ample that it just flowed into his mouth. She also felt that this is why she had menstruated since childbirth. A few other mothers have also felt that "an over-ample supply" might have been the cause of the early return of menstruation following childbirth. Hopefully the above suggestions—plus nursing lying down, which allows the baby to suck for a long period of time on one breast—will be helpful to these mothers.

"We Want to Avoid Thumb-Sucking"

Normally many parents have another purpose in mind besides pacifying when they offer the pacifier regularly to their babies. This is to avoid thumb-sucking and, possibly, any future orthodontic expenses. Dentists hold varying opinions on the matter. In 1961 an orthodontist at the University of California School of Dentistry in San Francisco taught us that (1) the young child should be encouraged to suck his thumb if he desires and that parents should not discourage this habit until after the child is four years old; (2) thumb-sucking will cause no harm to the permanent set of teeth if the child sucks up until four years of age; (3) the child's sucking needs are best satisfied at an early age when the child is allowed to suck as much as he desires; and (4) breast-feeding satisfies this need best. Many dentists now support the view that thumb-sucking does the child no harm until he is five or six years old, or until the time when his baby teeth begin to loosen. A few dentists will advocate "no thumb-sucking" because they feel that it will cause harm to the permanent set of teeth. Interestingly, some of these dentists also advocate "no pacifiers," since they feel that the prolonged use of either habit causes the same problems.

But no matter what view is held by a particular dentist or orthodontist, almost all are in agreement that sucking at the breast is better than sucking at bottles and pacifiers from the point of view of dental care. Breast-feeding also prevents tongue thrusting.[2] In addition, the stronger sucking that breast-feeding requires involves

2. Daniel Garliner, *Your Swallow: An Aid to Dental Health,* six-page pamphlet (The Gulf Building, Suite 715, 95 Merrick Way, Coral Gables, Florida).

a muscular action that is said to be very influential in the proper growth and development of the jaw, bones, and muscular tissues of the entire face. Studies also show that the presence of long-term nursing tends to decrease the need for orthodontic work. Thus, for those concerned parents, breast-feeding seems to be the first step toward preventive orthodontics. One must realize, of course, that orthodontic problems may arise from other factors that cannot be controlled by healthy sucking habits.

The relationship between the use of the bottle as a pacifier and tooth decay has also been highlighted in the daily press. In early December 1972 the New York Times Service reported that Dr. Stephen J. Moss, chairman of the department of pedodontics at New York University, told mothers to use bottles only at feeding times. The problem he saw was the repeated occurrence of extensive decay of the upper front teeth, which are surrounded or bathed by the milk or juice from the bottle.[3] What happens when the bottle is used as a pacifier is that the baby takes a couple of sucks and then swallows, but a little of the bottle's contents still seeps into the mouth and touches the teeth. An acquaintance of ours had this unpleasant experience to the tune of the three hundred dollars' worth of dental work that had to be done on her eighteen-month-old, bottle-pacified child. The child needed his four front teeth capped, and required both hospitalization and the service of an anesthesiologist, the fees of both of which, luckily were covered by insurance. The dentist explained that this decay was due to the lactic acid in the cow's milk used in the bottle-pacifier. But whatever the exact reasons may be, studies indicate that breast-feeding deserves considerable emphasis in a good oral hygiene program.[4]

PACIFIER PROBLEMS

Pacifiers may be dangerous objects, and the Food and Drug Administration is presently considering regulations with regard to their sale. Some tend to break into pieces, which could cut or choke the baby. One such piece caused a baby's death when it lodged in

3. *The Cincinnati Enquirer,* December 8, 1972.
4. Mary White, "Breastfeeding: First Step Toward Preventive Dentistry," *La Leche League News,* July–August 1972, p. 57.

30

his throat. Pacifiers are also a ready source of all sorts of germs, dirt, and other things. An acquaintance from Brazil told me that the mothers all nursed their children but that they also used bottles and pacifiers. He then spoke of the poor sanitation, and was especially concerned about the various types of worms the child could ingest by sucking on a dirty pacifier.

Pacifiers may create problems instead of solving them for the nursing mother. These difficulties were described in the La Leche League *Leaven* (May–June 1972) by a counseling mother.

It happened again, and I am finally moved to write. A mother called with a six-month-old baby on a nursing strike. Among other things I asked if she used a pacifier with her baby. I was almost sure the answer would be "yes," and it was. This is getting to be one of my routine counselling questions. When a mother with a one-month-old calls because her baby isn't gaining weight, or a mother calls because her three-month-old seems to be going through a growth spurt but will only nurse while the milk flows freely, nine times out of ten these babies suck long and frequently on pacifiers.

Perhaps I am so aware of this because heavy pacifier use was one of the downfalls in nursing our firstborn. He, too, nursed only for milk and got his main comfort from the pacifier. He would never nurse at length to build up a greater supply; during growth spurts I added extra solid food. By five months the nursing just petered out.

Even if the situation never gets this drastic, isn't one of the joys of nursing found in being your own baby's "pacifier"? To be able to soothe your little one at the breast when he needs this comforting form of love is one of the nicest inherent advantages of breastfeeding.

The absence of pacifiers may be very crucial in the maintenance of natural infertility. Nature provided the baby with his mother's breast and with his own fingers for satisfying his sucking needs. Artificial devices replace nature's products—and, as we have seen, the absence of natural baby care usually means the absence or shortening of natural child spacing. The two go together.

The following two stories show that total nutritional breastfeeding does not assure the absence of menstruation, as both mothers nursed totally for a considerable length of time and yet both experienced menstrual periods while doing so. However, their babies did use the pacifier regularly.

One mother had two periods while totally nursing. She told me this while her second child was cradled in her arms, sucking on a pacifier. We began to talk about pacifiers and how the babies are taught to suck on them instead of the breast; this was then related to the importance of the sucking act for the suppression of menstruation and ovulation. She said she had nursed her first baby, although not totally. Yet with him, up to the age of her present baby (about five months), she had not menstruated—and she never gave her first baby a pacifier.

Another friend, who nursed her baby for seven months before introducing solids, had experienced regular periods after childbirth. She nursed her baby every three and a half to four hours and offered him a pacifier so she "wouldn't have to nurse the baby all the time." Interestingly enough, this mother, after having several periods, then missed two periods during the time that she was expressing milk for another baby, in addition to feeding her own. Maybe this extra stimulation repressed her menses, for they resumed after she no longer expressed the extra milk for the other baby and was once again only providing for her own.

Does the pacifier make the difference? This is an interesting question, since the sucking, when limited to the baby's nutritional needs, does not seem to be effective in holding back menstruation in many cases. If the babies in the above stories had been pacified as well as fed at the breast, maybe this additional sucking might have been sufficient in suppressing menstruation.

THUMB-SUCKING

The absence of pacifiers automatically leads to the subject of thumb-sucking. This subject deserves more consideration and study with respect to mothering. Dr. James Clark Moloney, writing in *Child and Family* magazine,[5] discussed pathological thumb-sucking and attempted to show that the baby who sucks his thumb may be "mothering" himself; the thumb may become a substitute for the mother's breast and body. He explained how mother-body contact and free access to the breast provide satisfaction and reassurance

5. James Clark Moloney, "Thumbsucking," *Child and Family*, Summer 1967.

to the infant, and how such an infant has no need for a substitute. Noting other cultures, he told of the Okinawan mother, who places the baby at breast immediately after birth and continues to remain in close touch with him. The child is carried on his mother's back, and she caresses and cuddles him. The child sleeps on a mat with his parents. He is allowed to creep and crawl and explore on his own, yet he knows he can return to his mother's side any time he desires. The baby is so closely related to his mother that she senses his needs before he cries. He pointed out that unfortunately many American mothers tend to minister to their infants and then set them aside and leave them, treating them in what he called an undesirable arm's-length manner. Our culture tends to produce thumb-suckers, since maternal intimacy is lacking.

It is obvious that excessive thumb-sucking would have the same effect as a pacifier on the natural spacing processes in some cases, so some mothers have felt very strongly that the baby should not suck his thumb or fingers at all. I cannot be so strong about this issue. Some babies will suck their fingers often in spite of frequent nursing and close contact with mother. Babies may want to suck temporarily when uncomfortable—during a burping session or when teething, for example—and they will begin to suck upon awakening from their sleep, as the hunger develops. This sucking signals a need to the mother, who can then pick up the baby and offer the breast before he is fully awake and probably crying. Physical closeness makes the mother more aware of her child's needs—so much so that it might be said (and it has been suggested by other mothers) that *physical closeness* is a requirement for natural spacing.

Natural mothering, with its physical mother-baby closeness and unrestricted nursing, does not come easily in our society. With little outside support, most of us have learned the "art of mothering" through caring for two, three, or even seven babies. I admire and almost envy the young mother who has all this information before the birth of her first child. She can adopt this type of mothering right away, and receive the joys that come from it in her first effort. Some of us have felt that we did a good job of mothering only to discover that with our next child we were still doing things a bit differently. We mature and learn with each child. The difference may be slight, but it appears to be enough to eliminate the thumb-

	Child #1	Child #2	Child #3
PACIFIER	For only 3 months	None	None
BOTTLE	Gave 72 ounces during early postpartum weeks; mother had serious breast infections	None	None
SOLIDS BEGUN	At 6 months; with spoon	At 6 months; with spoon	At 9 months; with finger foods
CUP BEGUN	At 9 months; mother offered cup	After one year; on his own	After one year; on his own
NURSING COMPLETED	At 16 months	At 27 months	Still nursing often at 28 months
NIGHT FEEDINGS	First 6 months; then baby slept through	First 6 months; then baby slept through	Still nurses at night at 28 months
SLEEPING ARRANGEMENT AT NIGHT	In the crib	Mother nursed baby in bed but returned to crib	In parents' bed
PERIODS RESUMED	At 12 months postpartum	At 18 months postpartum	Never did; mother encouraged reduced nursings to achieve pregnancy, which occurred 27 months postpartum
THUMB-SUCKING	3 months to 4½ years	Began at 1 year and still does at 4½ years	Absent

sucking in some cases. The table opposite shows how three children were raised, each a little bit differently, by one mother.

May I quote the mother's remarks about thumb-sucking?

[Our first child] started sucking his fingers fairly early but I don't remember exactly when. He spontaneously gave this up when he was about four and a half years old or a little more. [Our second child] started sucking her thumb before she was a year old, and became quite an inveterate thumb-sucker. At four and a half she still sucks it a lot, chiefly at night or when tired or upset. I think our children must have a tremendous sucking need, and although I was more free in nursing this second child, and she in fact nursed a lot more than "average," it was obviously not enough to prevent the thumb-sucking. [Our third child] is far the most independent of our three, and the only one who has never sucked thumb or fingers. I have the feeling that if it weren't for so much nursing she would definitely have been a thumb-sucker. Occasionally I have seen her put her thumb in her mouth and start to half-suck, and then I would always pick her up for a nursing.

Her experiences tend to show a relationship between thumb-sucking and the amount of nursing and physical contact with mother. It is interesting to note that, as this mother gradually developed a more natural mothering style with each child, her length of infertility after childbirth increased.

It is not my intention to leave the impression that anything more than the tiniest bit of thumb-sucking will destroy the ecological balance. From my own experience, and from that of some other mothers, it is evident that a mother who adopts the natural mothering style may still have a baby who sucks his fingers or thumbs quite a bit without the mother having an early return of menstruation. It is likewise our experience that some thumb-suckers may grow to stop sucking on their hands and use only the breast for pacification at a much later date.

The point I am emphasizing, however, is that mothering practices in which the mother takes care of the nutritional and emotional sucking needs of the infant are those which reinforce the mother-baby ecology and tend to postpone the return of fertility and menstruation. The mother who adopts the philosophy of physical closeness and who has her baby physically near her at night as well as during the day is in a position to recognize the various sucking needs of her infant. When she satisfies these needs at the breast, she cooperates with the natural pattern. Offering the breast when she notices her baby sucking his thumb or fingers not only provides some milk and emotional comfort and reinforces the ecological relationship; it also may reduce or prevent a habit of thumb-sucking from birth or at a later date. Some of my correspondents have been quite emphatic on this whole subject, and some have stated their plans to offer the breast more with a future child when they see him sucking his thumb. The current reader has the choice and can benefit from our accumulated experience. It must be remembered, however, that some babies will at times prefer their fingers to the breast.

OTHER SOOTHERS

The child-care industry has come up with any number of things that can be used as mother substitutes. Used to excess, they not only interfere with the mother-baby ecology of breast-feeding and natural infertility; they can also hinder his development[6] and even lead to death from "unknown causes." For example, hospitals have found that infants need tender, loving care and that infants deprived of this care and physical contact will wither and not develop normally. We have heard the story of an orphanage where, some time ago, infants, kept in cribs, were given adequate nutrition and sanitation but where there was still a high rate of unexplained sickness and subnormal progress and development—except for the babies right near the door. Finally it was realized that the babies near the door were getting little bits of extra attention from nurses and maids as they came in and out of the door—patting them on the head, speaking to them, and so forth. A similar example is noted in "Of Babies, Beds and Teddy Bears" in the appendix of this book. From such examples we can see that even the crib or a playpen can be used in such a way that it becomes a prison instead of just a temporary protection against falling or getting hurt in some way.

I have heard of mothers who almost worshiped the infant seat. No one was permitted to pick up the baby, so a piece of plastic

6. Bonnie Prudden, *Is Your Child Really Fit?* (New York: Harper & Row, 1956).

became its habitual home. Perhaps one of the devices that is most easy to use to excess is the spring-wound swing. Just place the baby in the seat, wind it up, and baby may be content, almost hypnotically so, for literally hours. One former neighbor bragged about the fact that her baby ate and slept in such a swing. I don't think it requires much imagination to see how such baby-care practices may result in greatly reduced mother-baby contacts and breast-feeding, thus upsetting the ecology of breast-feeding and natural infertility.

Again, one's attitudes change. With our first baby we thought a playpen was an absolute necessity, but we actually rarely used it. We lost it in a move and never replaced it. Many devices are temporarily helpful to the mother, and even temporarily enjoyable to the baby. However, often their use can be called into question if the mother tends to rely on them. One device that is most helpful is the back carrier, which helps to provide the same type of closeness given by similar carriers among the more nature-oriented peoples of the world.[7]

7. Baby carriers are available at department stores, baby stores, and camping-outfitting stores. A homemade front sling for the baby is easy to make, and no sewing is required. Take 2½ yards of fabric 36 inches wide and tie the ends in a knot. The sling is worn over one shoulder and across the chest with the knot in back, and it can be taken on or off without untying the knot. Baby will fit securely in front, as the material tucks in tightly around his buttocks (his legs hang free) and offers support for his head. Extra material gathered around the baby's shoulders can be pulled up over his head to provide protection on an extremely windy or sunny day.

5

Schedules, Sitters, and Social Life

CHILD CARE: ADULT CENTERED OR CHILD CENTERED?

This chapter should make it very clear that the purpose of this book is not to teach women how to breast-feed *just* to have an extended period of natural infertility. Rather, I believe that ecological breast-feeding is part of a child-centered way of baby care. As such, it runs counter to the typical American culture, which is not child centered but, rather, is adapted to providing immediate convenience to parents. I stress the idea of *immediate* convenience, because it may well be that the short-term conveniences connected with early child care contribute to problems later on. For example, if properly breast-fed babies have ten times fewer allergy problems than bottle-fed babies, has the overall "convenience" of the bottle been worth it? Or, if women who have both bottle-fed and breast-fed tell me, as they have, that they have somehow developed a different, better, warmer relationship with their breast-fed babies, what might this mean in terms of the long-term relationship between mother and child?

Three indications of an adult-centered baby care are the attitudes and practices with regard to schedules, baby-sitters, and social life. Schedules are obviously for adult convenience, and the presence of baby-sitters means that mother and baby are being separated, possibly for long periods of time—thus upsetting the breast-feeding–child-spacing ecology. If a couple say that this baby isn't going to change in any way their active social life, it could hardly be more obvious that their whole way of life, including baby care, is centered around themselves as on-the-go adults. Such an attitude would most likely run into direct conflict with the baby-centered program that is essential for the natural mothering ecology.

We can't just drop out of our culture, but living within it doesn't mean that we have to adopt all of its practices. What I want to do in this chapter is to show how a natural mothering program of baby-centered child care is preferable to reliance on schedules and sitters; secondly, I want to offer some suggestions that can make social life quite compatible with natural mothering.

MOTHER AND BABY AS ONE

It is obvious that nature intended mother and baby to be one. In fact, a nursing mother who gives her total love and care to her baby will experience a relationship that she may never have with other persons. As one mother told me, "This is the first time I ever felt truly needed, that I was irreplaceable." This love relationship with its rewards is built in naturally—the mother's body is geared toward the giving by the continual production of milk; likewise the production of milk provides her with a mothering hormone, prolactin, that is not available to the nonnursing mother.[1] Nature has her own built-in laws for the child's development, and today her ways are being supported more and more by researchers in the field. For example, a chief ingredient for a healthy start in life is a continuous loving relationship with one mother figure. This nature has arranged through the oneness in breast-feeding. Contrary to the popular opinion that you should avoid spoiling a baby, we are now being told that you can't give the baby too much love. Love him, enjoy him, fulfill his needs, and respond to his smiles, cries, and discomforts. Nature helps babies to receive this constant, individualized attention through the breast-feeding relationship.

It appears that some of our cultural theories concerning child

1. Niles Newton: *Maternal Emotions* (New York: Hoeber, 1955) pp. 46, 50.

care lack common sense and feelings. Mothers are sometimes told that they should let their baby cry, that it is good that they frustrate the baby. The baby seems to be looked upon as a "thing" without feelings, almost lacking any human rights to be heard, understood, and loved. There are enough frustrations that occur naturally in everyday living without parents adding to them as a matter of policy.

Of course, all of this is done under the name of "not spoiling the baby." Spoiling a baby in this context refers to giving him attention of some kind when he cries or fusses. It is feared that he is just trying to get attention, which he doesn't really need, and is therefore being selfish. However, at his early age a baby's wants are simply the expression of basic human needs, both nutritional and emotional. A baby can't distinguish between legitimate needs and self-centered, unnecessary wants. When he fusses or cries, it is because he has a need that might very well be emotional rather than physical. Some writers have said that Mother Nature provided a built-in fussiness for babies so they will get some handling and comfort from their parents. Others have expressed concern about the good baby, who is never picked up. The point is that love demands that parents take care of their baby's needs, and you don't spoil a baby by taking care of his needs in a loving way. Natural mothering provides lots of personal contact, and is eminently well suited for taking care of a baby's needs.

SCHEDULES

Closely tied in with some faulty notions about not taking care of a fussy baby are some ideas about schedules. Some think that a baby should be put on a schedule so he will not manipulate his parents. It is feared that he will control the mother unless she controls him. He can even ruin family life and be a threat to a good marriage unless he is strictly scheduled and shown his place in the home! The emphasis here is on power rather than love. A baby has no complex ideas about controlling anyone. Nor can a baby and his needs be blamed for a deteriorating marital relationship. On the contrary, the sight of one's spouse going out of his or her way to take care of the baby's needs can be a source of renewed pride, but this is not to say that a baby is a cure for a poor marriage relationship. A baby has no plan for making people happy or unhappy.

Schedules simply have no place in natural mothering. In bottle-feeding, they serve the purpose of keeping babies from being starved by some mothers and overstuffed by others. However, in nature's baby-care plan, mother and baby are always together, and the mother very quickly senses her baby's nursing needs. This can contribute to the mother's self-esteem as she realizes her unique importance for her baby; it can also help develop her capacity for self-giving as she responds to his needs instead of scheduling him to fit her convenience.

Even a mother who remains with her baby must learn to ignore advice about schedules—unless, of course, there is a serious medical reason to do so. Today a nursing mother may be told that at such-and-such-a-time every day she will be feeding her baby and that by a certain age she will be feeding her baby only three or four times during the day. She might be told to nurse at least twenty minutes on each side. If she's in the hospital, she may be told that she can't nurse the baby until twelve or even twenty-four hours after childbirth, or that she can't nurse the baby every time it's hungry. While in the hospital she may be told to nurse only five minutes on each side and that's all! One friend told me that she was even told when she could bathe the baby, put it to sleep, and play with him. Obviously, such schedules are geared for adults and not babies. No consideration is given to the true needs of the baby—whether or not the baby is hungry or full, tired or sociable, dirty or clean.

Beginning at birth, the baby should be allowed to nurse as often and as long as he chooses. The popular four-hour schedule is not popular with breast babies. In fact, since breast milk is more agreeable to the baby's stomach and digests so much faster than other milks, many breast-fed babies will nurse twice during that amount of time. On occasion you may find yourself nursing your baby quite often, or even within the same hour. This shouldn't surprise us. After all, we adults often get up from the table only to find ourselves eating an hour later or drinking between meals. Nursing mothers generally comment that things run more smoothly once they accept the more frequent feedings and forget the clock

—and this applies even when the baby is older. In brief, rules are confusing because the schedule says one thing and the baby is telling mother something else. Mothering and breast-feeding are usually easier for both mother and baby when the mother takes her cues from the baby and learns to relax with this flexibility. From the preceding paragraph it should be clear why schedules would most likely upset the breast-feeding–baby-spacing ecology. The baby who is allowed to develop under the natural mothering program may be nursing every couple of hours during the day, sometimes even more frequently, thus giving his mother the frequent sucking stimulation that is necessary for her ovarian system to remain at rest.

BABY-SITTERS

The presence of a baby-sitter means the absence of the mother from her baby. This is not very easy in the natural mothering process, because the baby will need her presence for food at least within a couple of hours, if not sooner. Some mothers express their own milk, freeze it, and thus have it on hand in a bottle for the rare occasion when they just cannot be with their babies. The same holds true for the mother who simply cannot avoid having employment outside her home. However, basically natural mothering means that a mother is with her baby—and baby-sitters interfere with this type of mothering and therefore with the breast-feeding–baby-spacing ecology. Thus a mother who is interested in natural mothering and its related effect of child spacing will desire the oneness that nature intended between mother and child. She will soon learn that she does not desire to leave her baby; instead she finds that she wants to be with her baby no matter where she goes.

The problem, of course, with following the natural mother and baby togetherness is not the enforced separation of the working mother. (By the way, in some of the European countries, they have nurseries right at the place of employment so that mothers can be with their children occasionally during the day. A priest in Africa told us the working African mother has her baby right at her side. In America we have a long way to go.) The problem is basically a cultural thing that leads mothers to think that they need to be separated from their babies. There is a common expression of "being relieved of the baby." Many American parents make it a conscious goal to leave their children one or more times a week. It is considered necessary to do so in order to keep one's sanity.

Do other mothers require this relief from their babies? Dr. Thomas Lambo described the mothering customs of the African mother in an interview by James Breetveld for *Psychology Today*.[2] This psychiatrist says that the African mother is inseparable from her child during its first fifteen months after birth. The mother meets her child's needs freely and even anticipates them before the child begins to whimper. Gradually, the child is given over to other members of the family, who continue to give the child physical affection. Thus the child grows up in a secure environment of love and approval. The interviewer was interested in knowing if the African mother became irritated or annoyed with her child as a result of being with him continually. Dr. Lambo said that, unlike women elsewhere in Western cultures, the African mother exhibited very warm and affectionate feelings toward her baby and that breast-feeding plays a part in the mothering relationship. With increased urbanization, Dr. Lambo is concerned that this mothering pattern might be changed in Africa. He stated that when women become involved in two roles the traditional mother-infant relationship of inseparability undergoes a drastic change, and he is worried that this method of child care may be affected or lost to the African people. The report points out the fact that mothers can *enjoy* this oneness with their babies, that closeness and inseparability might play a big factor in this enjoyment, and that breast-feeding produces the environment for such closeness.

Another factor in this cultural advocacy of the separation of the parents from their baby is the mistaken idea that it is good for the baby to be exposed to a variety of people, the more the better, so that the baby will be social from the beginning. On the contrary, the baby needs its mother primarily, and, if an occasion does arise for a sitter, great pains should be taken to arrange to

2. February 1972.

have a familiar person take the mother's place. Dr. John Bowlby, in his book on maternal deprivation, *Child Care and the Growth of Love*,[3] states that parents should not leave any child under three for a matter of days unless for grave reason. If the mother must leave, a close neighbor or relative should take care of the child. He feels a stranger should not be chosen. Dr. Margaret Mead, writing on the subject of working mothers and their children,[4] warns mothers that frequent change in baby-sitters may be harmful to the child. She stresses the fact that a small child needs care continuously from one mother or mother-substitute.

STEPPING OUT WITH BABY

But to repeat an earlier statement, the mother of a new baby cannot simply drop out of society for three years. I doubt very much that the traditional African mother becomes a social recluse. The answer is as obvious as it is simple: mother takes her baby with her wherever she goes. However, such a simple solution seems to have two strikes against it. Many mothers feel culturally pressured not to bring babies with them in social gatherings; others wonder how they could take care of a nursing baby in public.

The problem of nursing in public is much easier to deal with than that of cultural pressures. The first is a matter of planning and techniques that will be explained shortly, but it sometimes takes conviction, courage, and character to stand up to the pressure of one's peers. In our society child care is a controversial subject itself, and unfortunately many mothers who feel right in what they are doing have been hurt by many unkind remarks. Some mothers have told me that they lost their best friends because of their differences with regard to child care. The mother who takes her baby with her to various places and social gatherings stands out as being different. The baby's presence says something about the mother's ideas about child care. It says rather clearly that she thinks that to bring her baby with her is anywhere from "good" to "the only way." Peer parents who have left their baby with a baby-sitter are prone to make judgments, and self-justification

3. Baltimore: Penguin Books, 1953.
4. *Catholic World*, November 1970.

may result in negative attitudes or judgments toward the mother-with-baby. Imagine the various currents and countercurrents when Couple A bring their baby to an evening at Couple B's house, only to find that Couple B have sent their children elsewhere to get them out of the way for the evening.

As the baby gets older, it gets even harder. As one friend said, "You only accept certain invitations, those where you know the baby is welcome. But, even when the baby is welcome, you know that the couples are wondering why you brought the baby, especially when he slept the whole time you were there. Yet, if the baby woke, I know how much he would need me."

You should be proud that you enjoy being with your baby and enjoy taking him places. You will find mothers complimenting you and saying, "What a good baby! Is he that good all the time?" As another friend said, "I hear these remarks so often when I go places with my baby that I begin to wonder if babies are all bad." You will also hear indirect comments from the mother, who will say, "I could never take my babies [or small children] anywhere even if I wanted to." In other words, your mothering and breast-feeding helps to tell the world that maybe there is a better way to raise babies, and that you don't have to be tied down while nursing!

If this is your first nursing experience, you may feel uncomfortable nursing in front of others. I certainly did! As I think back, I always had to leave to nurse in another room. There were times, however, when someone would say something positive about breast-feeding and encourage me to nurse in their presence. So I did, and I felt quite comfortable about it. As you nurse more and as your opinions and convictions about breast-feeding mature, you will find that you will be more and more comfortable with nursing outside the home.

The key to breast-feeding in the presence of people outside your immediate family is being discreet. Practice it at home, and you will soon find that your husband may not even know you are nursing when out! Actually, with proper clothing a nursing baby gives the appearance of being a sleeping baby. A mother can lift her blouse or sweater up a little from the waist and the baby's body will cover the exposed area. If you're wearing a blouse, it is usually easier to unbutton one or two of the bottom buttons. A knit top is great, since it stretches up where needed. And a blanket wrapped around the baby can be propped up in such a way as to provide a shield for the nursing area. Nursing can be so inconspicuous that no one has an inkling about what you are doing. There will be times when a person will ask to see the baby, thinking it's asleep. The baby may be asleep, but they will not realize when asking that it was at the breast.

Certainly, as a nursing mother you will want to consider the sensibilities of others. In a church service you may want to place your husband and other children between you and a complete stranger. Or sit on the aisle side of available seats, with your husband on the side where others would be sitting. If you visit a home where there are older children or teen-agers and you don't know the parents' attitudes about breast-feeding, it might be better to leave the room temporarily to nurse. There need be no explanations; just leave to use the bathroom with the baby.

Many nursing mothers feel that when female friends come over to visit they should be able to nurse in their own home as they normally do. Many have educated the neighborhood children as well about breast-feeding. When couples come to visit, again it's a matter of knowing how they feel about it. You may feel comfortable nursing in front of some couples when you entertain, and with others you will want to leave the room. I was always mad that I had to leave my own living room to nurse the baby. It presented me with a double standard: If I were bottle-feeding, I'd be quite welcome to my company.

One doesn't go against the cultural frown on public breast-feeding with ease, or overnight. It takes time, and, as I've already indicated, there may be some situations—either out in public or even in your own home—in which you may want to nurse privately. Still, you will generally find that, if you're quite casual, comfortable, and discreet about nursing in front of friends, they in turn will also feel comfortable. Other trends right now are making it even easier to buck the old taboos.

Every time I see girls and women showing off their breasts in revealing tops, I gain more confidence in doing what I feel is right with regard to nursing my baby. Why can these women draw approving glances for their detailed showing of the breast, while nursing mothers are frowned upon when they nurse their babies modestly in public without revealing the breast? Our society has a distorted view of the breast, and it's probably our number-one sexual hang-up. Hopefully, this attitude toward the nursing mother will change as society becomes re-educated about the values of mothering and the important role that the breast has for the baby.

Once a mother has decided that she's going to take her baby with her when she goes out, the rest is fairly easy. First, when nursing outside the home, it helps to have the right clothing. Two-piece outfits, dresses with hidden zippers near the breast area, pants suits, ponchos, and ruanas (heavy coat-length wrap-arounds with front opening for baby, ideal for cold climates) make nursing very easy. Never leave the home, even for a short time, in an outfit that makes nursing difficult, as baby might surprise you and you'll find you're not prepared.

Another tip for modest nursing is to wear bras that are easy to open with one hand. Some bras have snaps or hooks. Some nursing mothers prefer the bras with the "button" clip that can be easily opened with one hand. Since the most conspicuous part of nursing is getting ready or closing the flap, another idea is to wear a top you can't see through so one window flap can remain open. I often nurse on one side before we go out or before arriving, usually the right side. I can do more things nursing on the left side, and for some reason I prefer this side when I am out.

In the early months leakage can be a bit of a problem, but it can easily be managed. Nursing breasts sometimes get rather stimulated when out with baby, and in a short time milk has wet the bra and is making wet spots on your outer clothes. This can be a bit embarrassing sometimes, but there are a variety of solutions. The leaking can generally be stopped by applying pressure to the breast when you feel a let-down. This is obviously easier to do at home than in public, although you may fold your arms in a high position and apply pressure without anyone (except other nursing parents) knowing what you are doing. In another technique that goes unnoticed, I have at times applied pressure at one breast by placing my arm up toward the baby; the baby's body applies some pressure on the other breast. On some occasions a sports jacket or sweater may suffice to cover any leakage, while on other occasions you may want to use some pads inside your bra to absorb the leakage; homemade pads made from old cut-up diapers, hankies, klcenex, or other absorbent materials work well. During the early months when I go out, I usually leave a pad for protection only on the breast I am not using, and let my baby take care of the other.

Plastic wrap can also be used between the bra and your dress or blouse. Simply cut two pieces and tuck one in around the edges of each cup. However, the plastic cuts off all air circulation around the breast, and can lead to sore nipples or can aggravate nipples that are already tender or sore. Because this technique can cause these problems, I almost hate to mention it; but some mothers with heavy leakage may find this helpful, especially when wearing that favorite party dress that has to be dry cleaned. It need only be used for that special rare occasion, and it should never be used during a breast or nipple problem.

When going out, sometimes it helps to plan where you will sit before you arrive. There may be some areas in a particular building or home where you would feel more comfortable nursing. Take a restaurant, for instance. Maybe the husband and wife want to celebrate their anniversary; I have known several couples like ourselves who have taken baby or the family along. This is quite easy, providing you pick a place that has quick service as well as good food. Booths or out-of-the-way tables make it easy to nurse a young baby without being observed. A nice, dark atmosphere is not only romantic, but it might make for a more comfortable nursing situation. You may also want to select a place that has high chairs. The best advice to follow, of course, is to feed your baby if possible before arriving. If baby is sleepy and doesn't want to nurse, it may pay to wait until he nurses well and isn't tired before you take him out.

During the early months after childbirth it is helpful if the husband shops for groceries. To assist him, make easy shopping lists and let him do all the shopping in one store. When making the list, put the foods in the egg-milk-cheese section together or all the produce foods together, which will save him from making several trips back to the same part of the store. By going to the same market, he will become familiar with the best prices for certain products, and he will know where everything is, for faster shopping.

If a mother has only a few grocery items to buy, she can place her baby in an infant seat and then secure the infant seat into the front-seat section of the shopping cart. The baby would have to be very secure in the infant seat and under mother's careful watch. Some of the infant seats today are built larger and the width may not fit as suggested. When the baby is bigger and can sit up, the back carrier is very convenient to use while shopping. Common sense tells us that a hungry baby may soon turn fussy, so it's frequently a good idea to offer the breast in the car before taking him into a store.

Many mothers line up their baby's first baby-sitter when

they go for their first postpartum checkup. Again this is not necessary. Some mothers may feel comfortable nursing in the waiting room, especially if it is uncrowded or has other nursing mothers. Others may want to make use of one of the several other rooms in the doctor's office or even the patient's bathroom. Once in the examination room, the mother can hand her baby to the attendant nurse during the exam or use the baby bed some doctors provide.

Wherever you go there may be lounges, rest areas, dressing rooms, picnic areas, or isolated areas where nursing can be done easily if privacy is wished. If you have a car handy, this is also a convenient nursing spot. With proper clothing as suggested, you will find that once you gain confidence you may find yourself nursing along the sidewalk, on the school grass, at a picnic table, down mountain trails, or at the beach with a towel thrown over your shoulders. People will pass you by without notice. On your family outings, you will find that nothing is much more convenient than nursing in a car.

The portability of breast-fed babies makes them very adaptable toward social life, but certainly some forms are much easier than others. I would scarcely recommend taking a breast-fed baby to a symphony concert. But, when it comes to family outings, it would be hard to find a better traveler. Within three months of age, one of our babies had been on two overnight camping trips in a tent, a trip to the zoo, a week's trip to visit relatives, and two trips to the doctors, and there were many quick trips to the beach, picnic parks, and the nearby wading pool. When traveling to other countries, there is no concern about the water supply, and couples claim that when flying great distances by plane a breast-fed baby requires very little fuss.

While babies are great on family outings, there are other occasions when a mother knows that her baby would be unwelcome and it would seem best to try to avoid such situations. Let me put in here a personal plug for not using your breast-feeding as an excuse to avoid gatherings and events that you really weren't interested in anyway. It may be an easy excuse, but it certainly doesn't do much for the idea of the real freedom of movement that the breast-feeding mother enjoys. If you have to decline an invitation because you feel that the baby would be unwelcome, why not just ask if the baby is invited, too? Then explain that you are limiting your social life for a few months to those occasions when you can bring the baby.

The most difficult time will come when the baby is older and yet still needs you. There will be invitations that you will want to accept, yet will refuse because of the difficulty of taking an older baby. You will find that it helps to develop friends who have similar views and values and with whom your baby would be most welcome. An older baby may be nursed to sleep before the parents go out for the evening, but the mother should be prepared to come home immediately should the baby need her. Many older babies when mothered naturally will not take to sitters, even if the face is familiar. One of our children did not enjoy a baby-sitter until age three.

In summary, the ecology of breast-feeding–child spacing calls for that oneness of mother and baby that we have called natural mothering. Strict schedules interfere with this, and so do separations over an hour or so. Thus, it is best for a mother to follow the practice of the typical African mother mentioned previously. For the first twelve to fifteen months the mother and baby should be practically inseparable. The baby goes where mother goes.

PARENTAL RESPONSIBILITY

In all of this we have seen that breast-feeding and natural mothering do not confine a mother to the house or eliminate all social life. This is not to say that natural mothering does not make its special demands. Parents are mistaken when they try to act as if they weren't parents. The couples who continue to go away on weekends without the baby (or other children) or who keep up other life styles that consistently separate them from the baby or other children for long periods of time seem to forget that parenthood carries with it a new dimension—greater responsibilities and greater joys. This change can be compared to the change from the single life to the married life. There are more responsibilities, more adjustments, and hopefully more joys to be shared. The spouse who acts as if he were still single or who does as he pleases without consideration for his partner in marriage is immature. The parents who act without any consideration toward the new baby may likewise be considered immature. On the other hand, the couple who choose breast-feeding and natural mothering are showing a certain sense of responsibility toward the baby by trying to do what is best for him even when it causes certain changes in their own lives.

For many couples, perhaps breast-feeding is a blessing in disguise. Could it be that the abrupt severing of the physical relationship between mother and baby that is so common today is responsible in some way for the impaired relationship between many of our young people and their parents? We have all heard that the transition from the womb to life after birth is a shock to the infant. We have all heard of abandoned infants for whom the doctor's prescription was nothing more complicated or less demanding than lots and lots of loving care. The infant needs the loving presence of his mother, and this presence may sometimes entail her absence from a social event. If, however, the "presence demands" of breast-feeding are the occasion of providing a sounder psychological beginning for the infant, then what at first glance seems to be an infringement upon the parents' social life may very well turn out to be a distinct advantage for the child in terms of his later social life. Breast-feeding may also help the parents to develop the habit early of thinking in terms of what is best for the family or for the child. In later years, for example, a parent may find that staying home is again what is best for his teenager. Parents today complain that they don't know where their children are; as a matter of fact, teen-agers often don't know where their parents are. Much of the sexual abuse that occurs among teen-agers takes place at home when the parents are absent. Might breast-feeding teach parents something of the value of staying with their children and making the house a home by their presence?

6

Weaning and the Return of Fertility

NATURAL WEANING

The time has come when the baby will begin to wean himself from total nutritional dependence at his mother's breast to the stage where he is completely independent of her body as a food source. It is of interest to the mother who desires the most natural weaning of her baby and the benefits of natural child spacing to realize that there are different methods of weaning, and that one of these is quite conducive to natural child spacing.

In many quarters there is the practice of weaning a baby or toddler abruptly. One friend told me that she was advised to shorten the weaning process to one day. She was told by several acquaintances to refuse to nurse the child and let him cry it out. Presumably the baby would soon get tired of crying and take the bottle, which up to this time he had refused to take. Naturally, such a form of weaning would completely terminate any child-spacing effect that had been derived from breast-feeding and that might be continued for some time in a more gradual weaning process.

The natural means of weaning that can continue to maintain the child-spacing effect of breast-feeding is a very gradual process that is controlled largely by the baby himself. Although up to this point I have insisted that *total* breast-feeding is a very important factor to consider in order to achieve natural infertility, it is now necessary to point out that this form of gradual weaning at the right time may also lengthen the natural child-spacing effect.

It is just as important for the mother to wait until the baby is naturally *ready* for solids as it is for the mother to wean the baby *gradually* off the breast at the child's pace. Early weaning—by which is meant not only hasty weaning, but the early use of solids, bottles, or cups—by the mother may be gradual, but it is not what I call *natural* weaning. Nature apparently intended that the baby receive only milk from its mother in the first months of life. Any deviation from this natural plan, such as early weaning, usually brings with it a short history of breast-feeding. Short-term nursing among so many mothers today is why we hear the oft-repeated statement that women conceive while nursing. Early weaning means an early return of fertility after childbirth.

My own particular case points out the fact that gradual weaning alone is not sufficient to prolong the natural spacing effect *if* this gradual weaning occurs early, when the baby is still meant to have a milk diet from mother. With early weaning (use of the bottle, pacifier, and other practices not recommended in this book) I experienced menstruation three months after childbirth, even though I nursed for ten months and withheld solids until the sixth month. On the other hand, I found that by caring for a baby naturally (total nursing until the baby wanted other foods and nursing often to meet the child's emotional needs), menstruation returned around the baby's first birthday.

When natural weaning occurs, some babies may wean themselves rather quickly; others will continue to nurse quite heavily for a long period of time, even though they are eating many solid foods. Since it is the sucking stimulus that effects the body chemistry of natural infertility, *an older baby of increasing size, activity, and appetite may begin to take other food and still continue to nurse as much as before.* Frequent nursing may continue well into the second or third year of life.

If the baby is to set the pace, how can a mother tell when her baby is ready for his first taste of solid food? The answer is simple —the baby's actions will tell her when he is ready. A baby has an early desire to put everything into his mouth. There will come a time when the older baby, sitting on his mother's lap at the table, will not be satisfied until he can have some of the food that he sees in front of him. Or he will start to feed himself with his fingers when he is ready. The same holds true for the cup. Someday he will want a cup and will make his new desires quite evident. In other words, the mother does not spoon-feed a child or offer a cup in an effort to introduce baby to other foods or liquids. She waits and lets the child call the shots.

Normally, the child begins to show an interest in solids during the middle of the first year. A child is expected to show this interest at six months of age, although some mothers say their babies wanted solids at five and others at seven months of age or a little later. Some mothers have found that their babies take only a little bit of food at first, and don't really show a real interest in food until later. A mother may offer mashed banana or a mashed pea served on a baby spoon to her six-month-old only to find the baby pushing the food out of his mouth. The mother will then wait and maybe try again a few days or a week later. Some babies love to teethe or suck on clean chicken bones (large ones) or cold carrot sticks before they actually begin to swallow solid foods. Although most mothers have been taught by society that it is "good" for baby to eat lots of food three times a day right from the start, nature as usual seems to set a slower pace.

Now that the baby is showing an interest in food, the nursing mother can still be flexible to the baby's needs. Just as there was no rigid feeding schedule while completely nursing, so there will be no rigid feeding schedule during the weaning phase of breast-feeding. She may offer him a little food once or twice a day; another day she may be surprised to find that her baby only nursed the entire day. Gradually, however, he will be at the table for most of the family meals.

The mother who is nursing has not had, of course, the mess of spoon-feeding a young infant, nor the problem of cleaning bibs or stained shirts. She will find now that feeding solids to an older baby is very easy. At the table the mother can mash the food with a fork, and certain foods, such as fresh fruit, can be scraped with a spoon. The mother will discover that her baby soon prefers his food in strips. These finger foods can be made from a variety of nutritious foods (hot dogs, liver, moist ham, cheeses, cooked egg, vegetables, fruits). She will not offer her baby sweet foods of the candy and cookie variety. She will avoid excess use of filler foods such as processed white bread and crackers. These foods may decrease the baby's desire to eat good foods, and they may be harmful to the baby's teeth.

It should be remembered that the beginning of solid food does not mean an end to breast-feeding; *solids at first are only a supplement to breast-feeding and not a replacement.* Nursings will still be periodic and frequent if the baby desires them ·'ay or night. The baby may still want to nurse during the night or upon awakening in the morning. He may want his mother at the table during and again after a meal. The mother may be offering the breast for a mid-morning or a mid-afternoon snack, and her baby will probably still want to be nursed to sleep. Breast milk will still continue to be an easy, quick nutritious food for the thirsty or hungry toddler. It will continue to be his liquid diet for many months. After he shows some interest in a cup, he will continue to nurse at the breast and may frequently insist on having a drink from his mother while flatly refusing any cup she offers him.

Babies will naturally wean themselves off the breast without any coaxing or prodding from their mothers. A few babies finish weaning before their first birthdays, but this is early. Most babies wean before or after their second or third birthday. Many people are upset to hear that a one-year-old is still nursing, but think nothing of a two-year-old with bottle in hand. Thus, when someone expresses surprise at a baby still breast-feeding past his second or third birthday, the nursing mother might politely ask if her friend would be surprised if the baby had an occasional bottle or used a pacifier at that age. Toward the end of the weaning period it must be remembered that the child is not nursing every few hours, but may be nursing only occasionally during the day—for example, before going to sleep or during the night. The night feeding is often the last feeding to be dropped.

There are a few other points I would like to bring up with respect to natural weaning. First, it would be wrong for a mother to withhold solids selfishly at her baby's expense or health. She should not consider prolonged 100 percent breast-feeding in order to prolong the absence of menstruation for a longer period when her baby really wants and needs solid food. Secondly, natural weaning does not mean that she will hold her baby back. A mother can't help but offer her baby encouragement over his progress. On the other hand, she will also realize that this older child is still a baby in many ways and he will still need her. Neither will she deprive him of this need in order to achieve another pregnancy. She accepts this "nursing" need of his approvingly and learns to enjoy this long-term relationship.

Niles Newton in her book *Maternal Emotions*[1] concludes from her studies that what counts in a nursing relationship is the *type* of breast-feeding and the *type* of weaning. Unsuccessful breast-feeding is that type of breast-feeding in which the mother calculates, regulates, and weighs the nursing experience. She constantly worries about her milk, when to give it and how long to give it. The nursing is so limited that more breast problems develop. Weaning comes early as a result of all the bother. Successful breast-feeding is different. The mother feeds the baby as he desires. The milk is plentiful, there are no worries, and the mother enjoys the relationship with few breast problems. The unrestricting approach of this type of breast-feeding is more enjoyable, and thus the mother is in no hurry to end the nursing relationship. In addition, Niles Newton questions whether the baby may be hurt by sudden weaning, as this means an abrupt ending to a close, intimate relationship with the mother. Thus, gradual weaning might be best for both the mother and baby, since the change comes slowly.

RETURN OF MENSTRUATION

During the natural course of breast-feeding a mother will experience the return of menstruation, for during the weaning process the baby will be taking less and less from the breast. This reduction in the sucking stimulus is what causes the return of menstruation, for the sucking stimulus no longer has sufficient influence over the reproductive system.

If the weaning process is a natural affair, the return of menstruation will usually occur while the mother is nursing her baby. If the weaning is abrupt, the return of menstruation normally occurs

1. New York: Hoeber, 1955, p. 49.

several weeks (two to six) after the nursing has stopped. Any sort of weaning, then, brings with it the eventual return of menstruation.

The first sign of the future return of fertility is generally what we have been talking about, the return of menstruation. I say "future return," because ovulation does not usually occur before the first period following childbirth. Many nursing mothers have relied successfully on breast-feeding during amenorrhea, and some mothers have experienced some infertile cycles after the return of menses. On the other hand, some nursing mothers have conceived without a return of menses. Present research seems to indicate that the risk of pregnancy prior to the first menses is about 6 percent.

The absence of menstruation provides a sense of security for the nursing mother who would like to avoid an immediate pregnancy following childbirth. This feeling of security can be lost if any bleeding or spotting occurs. Some mothers experience spotting or bleeding in the early months, but then increase the nursings to hold back menstruation once again. Spotting may also be a warning that menstruation or ovulation is just around the corner. Indeed, a few mothers have conceived after a spotting and without having had a regular menses. For mothers who do not desire another pregnancy and are concerned about the risk of pregnancy prior to the return of menstruation, proper information about the mucus discharge that occurs prior to ovulation or the first postpartum menses can be extremely valuable.[2]

Nursing mothers whose menstrual periods have not returned may be confused when they experience bleeding that is not menstrual in nature. The bleeding can be due to other factors. For example, one friend who had not expected her periods to return until the baby was about a year old experienced several days of bleeding. She then remembered that the bleeding occurred after a Pap test was taken; she had been told that the bleeding was a normal result of the Pap test. The bleeding stopped, and her periods did not return for months.

Another friend began cauterization treatments for cervical erosion. This "treatment" bleeding does not bring on a period, but

2. See pages 180–181.

58

it is confusing to the nursing mother who has not had any periods. The amount of bleeding varies considerably. For example, this mother bled seven days after the first treatment and twenty days after the second treatment. She was told that this "treatment" bleeding was all within the normal range. With such a lengthy flow, a mother can become concerned as to whether the bleeding is due to menses or the doctor's treatment.

The return of fertility does not mean an end to nursing. A mother can continue to nurse her baby or child while menstruating and even while pregnant. Many doctors become upset about the latter situation, but some mothers will continue to nurse in spite of their doctor's protest. It has been done for centuries, and has not yet been proven harmful to the unborn infant if the mother has an adequate diet. Weaning, however, may occur naturally during a pregnancy. The circumstances may change during pregnancy, and either the mother or the baby will want to give up the nursing relationship. The mother may physically resent the nursing due to hormonal changes, even though she had planned to nurse throughout the pregnancy. She may feel uncomfortable due to tender breasts or other physical changes, although some mothers will continue to nurse in spite of the discomfort because their child is not ready to wean. If a mother is uncomfortable with nursing, her child might accept brief feedings or reduced nursings if a good substitute such as back rubs is offered. The child may react to the changes in the milk during pregnancy; it tastes different, and he may lose interest.

Some mothers continue to satisfy the child's needs at the breast while pregnant and continue to nurse two following childbirth. This is especially true in other cultures where breast-feeding is widely practiced. Several mothers have found that continued nursing is desirable from the standpoint that the older child does not resent the new baby. One mother wrote of her older nursing child:

Her complete acceptance of nursing as a fact of life for herself and for the baby is as delightful and useful a thing as amenorrhea—in that jealousy in its usual forms with the birth of a new baby has been minimal; any reaction has been more like intrigued attention at odd moments. That's been particularly refreshing to me, since our first early-weaned child was a most unhappy soul for ages, when faced with a similar situation. So not only did I enjoy a completely successful two-year spacing between children, but also this added bonus of a happy displaced toddler.

A nursing mother when pregnant should consider the consequences of her actions. Is her child ready for reduced nursings? Do other activities with mother suffice in place of a nursing? Many nursing children, even the older ones, will not be ready to wean; and, if so, there is really no reason to quit. Actually, as we have seen from the above example, forced weaning may be most unpleasant after the birth of the newborn, whereas continued nursing may be advantageous under the circumstances. In addition, a child who has had his needs fully met by his mother and who knows his mother will continue to satisfy his needs and love him will be less inclined to be jealous, since he has a secure relationship with his mother and the new baby does not pose any threat to that security. He is also more inclined to be concerned that the baby gets *his* needs met, too. There is nothing more touching than to see a young brother or sister be upset at the first cry of the new baby and insist that Mommy take care of baby right away.

I have also received a few letters from mothers who quit nursing during pregnancy because they felt they should. Later they were upset to hear that they could have continued the nursing. One such mother, who had a stillborn, regretted her weaning decision during early pregnancy. A mother likewise may wean and later experience a miscarriage. Breast-feeding will not affect a good pregnancy, but such situations do happen whether one is nursing or not, and thus these possibilities are worth considering when making a decision. On the other hand, these considerations should not lead a mother to feel forced to continue nursing during pregnancy. She should feel free to do what she sees as best, everything considered.

MENSTRUAL VARIATION AMONG MOTHERS

Why does one mother nurse her completely breast-fed baby and have periods while another mother introduces juices early and still does not experience a menstrual period? Why does one mother whose baby uses a pacifier regularly not experience a period until her nursing baby is two years old while another mother follows all the rules for natural mothering and experiences a period when her child is five months old? Apparently the amount of mothering and stimulation required at the breast to hold back menstruation seems to vary among mothers, some of whom require more stimulation than others.

There is also some evidence that the older a woman is, and the more children she has had, the longer it will be before menstruation returns. However, this increase in amenorrhea is so small that one wonders if the experience built up over the years creates more confidence and, as a result, mothers nurse better and longer with each child. Better and longer lactation would tend to postpone menstruation a little longer. On the other hand, a few mothers have experienced an earlier return of menstruation with advancing age. These mothers have nursed other babies, yet with their new baby they are disappointed when menstruation returns earlier than ever before. Some mothers who were following the guidelines in this book have told me this has happened to them.

Likewise, babies vary. Each baby has different sucking and weaning needs; some babies desire the breast oftener than others. These factors are individual variations over which we have little control. However, they appear to be minor considerations for most mothers.

The most important considerations are those over which we have a great deal of control. Are we going to care for our babies at the breast naturally or are we going to nurse but also offer breast substitutes? Are we going to follow the total mothering program? This is what will make the difference to the individual mother. Here is an example from a mother who used only breast-feeding to space the births of her children. The first baby was nursed for eleven months (totally breast-fed for five), had night feedings for eight months and used a pacifier frequently; menses returned at six months and conception occurred at twelve months postpartum. With the second baby the mother nursed for twenty-six months. Solids were offered at six months, but the baby did not take them until seven or eight months. This baby never had a pacifier and was given night feedings until twenty-six months of age. Menses returned at twenty-four months and conception occurred at twenty-five months postpartum. As we see here, a change in mothering practices can affect the duration of amenorrhea for an individual mother.

For many mothers the mechanism involved is a very delicate one. Any decrease in the nursing may cause a return of menses. Eliminating one guideline from this book then may shorten or eliminate any natural-spacing plan for a particular woman. These mothers require lots of stimulation to hold back menstruation. Mothers who are giving total nutritional breast-feeding and who have experienced the return of fertility or menses are usually— but not always—not following the natural mothering program. One mother, for example, stated that she was totally breast-feeding and nursing her baby "all the time" when her periods returned. Upon further discussion it became clear that the mother fed the baby during the day only about once every four hours and the baby was already sleeping through the night.

The mothers who require lots of stimulation will probably find that, once their periods return, they will continue to have periods regularly even though the baby may increase his nursing at the breast. However, there are other mothers who require very little stimulation to hold back menstruation. They can be down to only two nursings a day and still not experience a return of menses. In addition, once their periods do resume, a little bit of increased nursing at the breast may influence their cycles. Increased nursings —for example, when the baby is sick—may delay ovulation in a cycle; thus the cycle would be longer than usual. Increased nursing may also inhibit the cycles so that the mother does not experience menstruation again for a length of time. This type of suppression is more likely to occur during the first year after childbirth and less likely to occur after a year of nursing.

This type of menstrual disturbance is less likely under the natural mothering program, since the stimulation is gradually reduced and coincides with the baby's reduced sucking needs. The natural return of menstruation via natural mothering tends to provide more regularity for the nursing mother. Cultural nursing, with its use of artifacts as mother substitutes, usually results in a fairly early return of menstruation. For various reasons, including the variations in the young baby's sucking pattern, delayed and irregular periods appear to be more commonly associated with an early return of menstruation than with a later return.

What if you are an exception? Exceptions occur, but they are few in number. This can be a great disappointment to a mother who desires the spacing or the absence of menstruation. This mother needs to accept herself as she is, and hopefully she will soon lose the feeling of disappointment. Here is a quote from one such mother: "After each birth, in spite of frequent nursings, late solids, no bottles, prolonged night feedings, no pacifiers and so on, my periods always return by four months, and the longest I have gone without conceiving is nine months." Another mother wrote me for the second time and said:

I know that we have already agreed I am a special case, but I thought I'd pass this information along to you anyway. Increased sucking helps to stave off periods? Well, our newborn son is now two months old and I've just had my first period—the earliest, I think, I've ever had periods return. In addition to nursing the baby, I'm also nursing our twenty-two-month-old and am collecting at least three ounces of milk a day for a sick baby! I'm disgusted with the malfunction of my body!

Another mother inquired and discovered that her maternal grandmother had also experienced early menstruation while nursing. These cases illustrate that a few mothers will experience an early return of menses in spite of the presence of natural mothering. They can expect a temporary disappointment, but hopefully they can go on from there, accepting the fact that this is their own natural pattern.

Generally speaking, when can fertility be expected to return? Our research[3] shows that women who adopt the natural mothering program will *average* 14.6 months without periods following childbirth. This is only an average. Some, an exceptional few, will experience a return before 6.0 months postpartum. Others will go as long as 2.5 years without menses while nursing.

Some mothers who are well informed about natural family planning and fertility awareness have found that even when periods return early, they charted many infertile cycles with continued fre-

3. See pages 163–175.

quent nursing. Thus for these mothers fertility is delayed, even though menstruation is occurring regularly.

Those mothers who go for two years without a period are on the long side of the average in our study, but they are not abnormal; indeed, there is some indication that such extended lactation amenorrhea is common in some cultures. One study among the Eskimos showed that the mothers who nursed traditionally did not conceive until twenty to thirty months after childbirth, whereas the younger mothers who adopted the American practices of supplements and bottle-feeding were conceiving within two to four months after childbirth.[4] When I first wrote this book I felt that a lactation amenorrhea of twelve months was exceptionally long. Since that time I have met quite a few mothers who have experienced amenorrheas of longer duration, so that 24 to 30 months without a postpartum period sounds very normal.

It is generally thought that the saying that a woman cannot get pregnant while nursing is an old wives' tale or superstition. Doctors commonly express this view. I agree that a woman can get pregnant while nursing; however, this fact does not present the whole story. With the typical American pattern of restricted nursing, fertility returns quite quickly—frequently just as quickly as for the nonnursing mother. On the other hand, with proper knowledge and support, with the adoption of the natural mothering program, the average nursing mother will experience an extended period of infertility. If no form of birth regulation is used except natural breast-feeding, babies on the average will be born about two to three years apart.

4. J. A. Hildes and O. Schaefer, "Health of Igloolik Eskimos and Changes with Urbanization" (Paper presented at the Circumpolar Health Symposium, Oulu, Finland, June 1971).

7

The Ecology of Natural Mothering

Our attention is often drawn toward the science of ecology and its importance in developing a better world for tomorrow. Man is learning that there is a balance in nature, and that when he interferes with this balance there can be some serious side effects. The environmentalists express their concerns about some issues that affect each one of us. These issues are (1) quality of life, (2) pollution, and (3) population. The environmentalists hold varying opinions on each issue, yet very few have probably considered how breast-feeding could be an "ecological" approach that has wide implications. In all three of these areas our environment could be improved by heeding that most basic form of ecology between mother and baby—breast-feeding. Ecological breast-feeding has many advantages, not only for mother and baby, but also the wider environment in which they live.

Here it is assumed that ecological breast-feeding means that type of natural mothering described in this book. It excludes that type of breast-feeding commonly observed in our culture which is associated with bottles, pacifiers, mother substitutes, strict schedules, abrupt weaning, and so forth. Secondly, the mother-baby ecology is not limited to breast-feeding, although breast-feeding will be our main concern here. It is obvious that this mother-baby ecology begins at conception, and that it can be disturbed prior to or at the time of birth by man's tamperings. More will be said later with respect to chidbirth as this event can influence the breast-feeding ecology.

One of the examples of ecology most familiar to naturalists is the relationship between the rhinoceros and the tick bird. The bird does the rhino a double favor—feasting on the ticks that bother the rhino and sounding an alarm whenever something approaches. This points up one of the basic facts of ecology: both partners in a natural relationship benefit from it. In the breast-feeding ecology it's not the baby alone who benefits; the mother has her share of blessings also.

QUALITY OF LIFE FOR THE CHILD

No matter what formula and baby-food ads would like us to believe, research[1] still shows us that babies thrive best on mother's milk. What happens when man adopts the "scientific" methods of infant feeding? Dr. Otto Schaefer recently studied the effects of urbanization upon the Eskimos and found that the bottle-fed children had a higher incidence of gastrointestinal diseases, respiratory and middle-ear diseases, and anemia compared to the traditionally breast-fed youngsters. He feels strongly that bottle-feeding is related to a very common health problem among children—chronic ear infection. In addition, he states, "Changing infant nutrition practices and the extraordinary perversion of the female breast from a nutritional organ to a sex symbol, which is so typical in Western civilization, has affected the individual's health far beyond infancy, as the markedly higher incidence of allergic and auto-immune diseases in bottle-fed than in breast-fed children suggests."[2]

In the poorer areas of the world bottle-feeding has already been introduced, and the protection afforded the baby through breast-feeding has been eliminated. It is known that in these poorer areas, where sanitation and food are lacking, the breast-fed baby has a lower death rate than the bottle-fed baby. More and more doctors are beginning to express their feelings concerning the value of

1. D. B. Jelliffe and E. F. P. Jelliffe, "The Uniqueness of Human Milk," *The American Journal of Clinical Nutrition* 24 (August 1971): 968–1024.
2. Otto Schaefer, "When the Eskimo Comes to Town," *Nutrition Today*, November–December 1971, p. 16.

breast-feeding in these countries for reasons of nutrition, health, and cost.[3]

How does infant technology affect the child emotionally? We now know that a child can suffer according to the degree of maternal deprivation he has experienced during the first few years of life. He may receive the best of physical care with respect to his body, but if he lacks a mother or mother-substitute he does not have the best start in life. An infant thrives on love, security, and intimacy from his mother. By being held, cuddled, and kept in frequent touch with his mother, the child has a richer start than the child who is left with many baby-sitters or allowed to spend hours in an area without the close presence of mother. Maria Montessori in her book *The Absorbent Mind* stresses the need for mother-baby oneness:

But let us think, for a moment, of the many peoples of the world who live at different cultural levels from our own. In the matter of child rearing, almost all of these seem to be more enlightened than ourselves—with all our Western ultramodern ideals. Nowhere else, in fact, do we find children treated in a fashion so opposed to their natural needs. In almost all countries, the baby accompanies his mother wherever she goes. Mother and baby are inseparable.[4]

An American mother writes explaining how she became impressed with a form of mothering she had not witnessed in her own country:

As a college student I majored in intercultural studies and realized many of our child-rearing practices did not seem as successful for either mother or child as those in many non-Western countries . . . at least in their traditional cultures. I traveled in Africa one summer and, even though a baby of my own was the farthest thing from my mind, I couldn't help but notice how happy and content all the babies and small children seemed, though I'm certain the general nutrition of their families was usually inadequate. The babies were almost always carried

3. Alan Berg, "The Economics of Breast-Feeding," *Saturday Review*, May 1973, pp. 29–32. The article provides an excellent short treatment of the dollar and human costs of bottle-feeding on a world-wide basis. (The article is adopted from *The Nutrition Factor*, The Brookings Institution, 1973.)

4. Trans. Claude A. Claremont (New York: Dell, 1967), p. 104.

on their mother's backs and children and mothers were together. These facts stayed with me and influenced my attitudes toward our family.

In societies where mother and baby are separate, the rationalization that crying is "good" for a baby seems to develop. Dr. Lee Salk and Rita Kramer discuss this aspect of child raising in their book *How to Raise a Human Being*. Here are their comments:

There's no harm in a child crying; the harm is done only if his cries aren't answered.

Babies who are left to cry for long periods of time and are overwhelmed by frustration develop neurotic behavior, in extreme cases even become psychotic. If you ignore a baby's signal for help, you don't teach him independence. How can a helpless infant be independent? What you teach him is that no other human being will take care of his needs.[5]

There are many sayings telling the mother that if her baby receives hate, he will learn to hate. Or if her baby receives love, he will learn to love. This was the basic message of Selma Fraiberg in her *Redbook* article, "How a Baby Learns to Love."[6] She also explains beautifully why the older baby resents a stranger or the separation from mother. Unfortunately, in our society many babies are not learning how to love. They are constantly yelled at, spanked, and shoved around at the will of their parents. And because these children received such treatment, it is likely that they, in turn, will treat their "loved" ones, their spouse and children, in a similar manner. The cases of child abuse are on the uprise, and the evidence shows that the overwhelming majority of these battered children were "wanted" children.

Am I hinting that breast-feeding is going to change all this? No, not automatically, but I seriously think that breast-feeding "the natural way" can bring about many changes. One mother told me that she has only spanked her breast-feeding children once or twice, yet she often spanked her bottle-fed children when they were younger. She felt that she has a greater understanding or sensitivity to their needs, that she is experiencing a special bond with her breast-fed children. Another mother said she felt she would be rougher with her child if she didn't breast-feed. In other cultures where breast-feeding is common, it is noted that the

5. New York: Random House, 1969, p. 65.
6. May 1971.

mother does not hit her child violently, and yet she disciplines. *National Geographic* carried an article by Kenneth MacLeish and John Launois, "The Stone Age Men of the Philippines,"[7] which describes a society in which affection is the permeating force and violence is lacking. The article notes that the women breast-fed for several years and that the mothers are firm when disciplining their children but do not spank them.

In the oneness relationship found in breast-feeding, how can the mother strike or be violent with her child? It is as unlikely as a mother who would strike or mishandle herself. Lucky indeed is the child who is nursed for several years, for his mother will probably have a close relationship with him that will remain even after the breast-feeding days are gone. He will be loved, and his mother will have learned easily how to respect his needs and his person during the years to come.

Breast-feeding provides a wonderful opportunity for physical contact between mother and baby. The importance of a mother's loving touch has especially been revealed in some difficult cases, where it has apparently resulted in startling improvements in the child's behavior.

In one case a baby approached death as his blood sugar level dropped to zero soon after childbirth. With emergency care he survived, but it was believed that brain damage had occurred. The parents, however, were encouraged by their doctor, who explained that with the best of care the brain, especially of a newborn, could be reprogrammed.

After a two-week stay in the hospital, the baby—who could just lie there, having lost almost all the responses normal to a small baby—was allowed to come home. Even though he sucked poorly from the bottle filled with breast milk, the mother gradually taught him to nurse at the breast. But what is most impressive is the beautiful care this baby was fortunate enough to receive. The mother says:

In addition to the breast-feeding, David always slept with me, and was constantly carried, either in my arms or in a Happy Baby Carrier on my chest. Every evening, after the other children were in bed, I would take off all his clothes and play with him, caressing every part of his

7. August 1972.

body, particularly his head. He also had a leisurely bath each morning, during which there was a great deal of physical contact. Gradually he began to respond and cry and react like a normal baby.

Upon pediatric examination and neurological testing at five months of age, the child, who had been fed on mother's milk only, was found to be completely normal, and there was no evidence of permanent brain damage. The specialists could not believe that this was the same child who had been so sick as a newborn.[8]

Does nature have the answer to child care? It may be worth a try. More writers are stressing the importance of the first few years of life—the importance of the mother-baby relationship, the importance of the mother responding to her baby's cries or fussiness and loving him dearly without fear of spoiling him. On the contrary, they stress the fact that many babies did not receive enough cuddling and holding. This seems to be the one time in a child's life when the mother cannot hurt him by giving her all. In fact, giving her all is what mothers are increasingly being encouraged to do. And this has been nature's plan for years.

QUALITY OF LIFE FOR THE MOTHER

The mother's own health benefits from breast-feeding. The breast-feeding mother reduces her chance of developing breast cancer; the greater the number of children nursed and the longer the nursing period, the more protection is afforded. Breast-feeding is the natural method of releasing the placenta after birth. A nursing mother does not experience the "after-childbirth blues," since her hormones are still riding high. Nor will she experience a similar fate later under the natural weaning program, since the hormonal changes occur very gradually. A nursing mother also regains her prenatal shape, especially her internal organs, faster, and in a few cases breast-feeding may prevent surgery. One such lucky mother from Australia wrote as follows:

I suffered a third-degree prolapse of the uterus after the birth of our fourth child. The doctor suggested at only three weeks, then again

8. Donald Parker, "David's Story," *La Leche League News,* March–April 1971, p. 22. Similar accounts are related in other issues of the *News*: Maybach, Minnesota *News* insert of November–December 1971; Ryan, *LLL News* of July–August 1968.

at six weeks, after birth that I arrange immediately for surgery. I declined on the grounds that it would force weaning onto the baby as well as upset the general family balance. When he saw my reason was genuine, he agreed with my course of action and told me to grin and bear it as long as I could. Well, after four weeks the symptoms ceased to be hurtful and I gradually forgot its presence. At ten months I had occasion to have another doctor do an examination of the cervix. Out of curiosity I asked for his comment on the prolapse; it turned out to be virtually disappeared. He heartily agreed with my suggestion that breast-feeding was the main help in restoring the sagging sinews and muscles to original condition.

It is a well-known fact that nursing often after childbirth is nature's way of contracting the uterus back to its original size. The shots and pills given after delivery for this purpose are normally not necessary for the alert nursing mother.

It is also known that women have a higher iron requirement due to their monthly menses. Television ads frequently encourage women to take iron pills to maintain health and energy. Again, with good nutrition and natural mothering these pills would largely be unnecessary. Through the prolonged absence of menstruation following childbirth a woman regains her bodily store of iron, which would otherwise be lost through menstrual flow. As usual, if we look to nature we will find an answer, and thus lactation amenorrhea is a health asset to the mother in her child-bearing years. Breast-feeding not only eliminates the need for drugs under

normal situations, but it may also be a form of preventive medicine, for diseases such as breast cancer.

Another physical aspect that is often forgotten in our busy world is the tranquilizing effect that nursing has on a woman. It provides brief rests during the day, and this form of relaxation can be a "plus factor" for the mother who tends to be tense and nervous. In addition, her body is producing prolactin, a "mothering" hormone that bottle-feeding mothers don't have. Thus, the nursing mother is not only *thinking* of being a good mother, but her body is producing the mood and she is *feeling* it as well.

Can breast-feeding be emotionally satisfying and provide fulfillment to the mother within the home?

Today women's liberation is a popular discussion topic, and one of the big pushes within the movement is to encourage women to seek fulfillment outside the home. In fact, many articles claim motherhood is a myth or that a woman "should" or "must" seek fulfillment outside the home if she is to be happy, if she is to maintain a happy marriage, and so on. It is implied that if a mother cannot be successful in the working world, she will also be a failure at home. Husbands are encouraged to share their career days with their wives by arranging days when they will also help with the baby, feed the older children, and do housework.

One wonders how much of this fits in with the research work done in the area of child care. Will the "two-parent" mother be better than the "one-parent" mother? If we look at nature, we find that breast-feeding clearly defines who is primarily responsible for the child. This is not to suggest that husbands shouldn't share in diaper changing, washing dishes while mother is nursing the baby, rocking or walking the baby to sleep when he doesn't want to nurse, and so on. It appears, however, that nature intends the mother to have primary responsibility in the early years.

It appears to me that women's liberation has emphasized for years the *mother's* liberation that occurred via the bottle. Mothers looked to the bottle as a way of liberation; it was to free the mother to go more places and do more things. And so the bottle became popular. The baby also became less and less happy, and soon toys and equipment were resorted to in an effort to entertain the baby while mother was being entertained elsewhere. Others rationalized this mother-baby separateness by the "crying-it-out" theory. What has developed is a society in which parents go out of their homes, completely disregarding the fact that they are parents. Go to any women's or mothers' clubs or organizations (except for groups that promote the natural, such as childbirth or breast-feeding) and you will hardly find one mother with her baby. Yet, if mothers read what is being written today, they should have their babies with them regardless of the method of feeding chosen.

Actually, "bottle-centered" mothering or the cultural-type mothering of our present day has liberated women too much from the satisfaction they should naturally derive from being a woman and mother. The bottle has taken many of her womanly privileges away from her; it has taken away some of the pleasures of mothering. In addition, it has increased the chances of sickness for her baby, taken away the natural infertility designed for her by nature, caused her more work, and cost her more money. Ask any mother who has bottle-fed and breast-fed what the difference is between the two methods. I have yet to hear anyone with both experiences rave about the bottle method. The more naturally a mother cares for her baby, the more inevitable it becomes that she will derive enjoyment from it.

What truly liberates the woman is natural or ecological breast-feeding. What she needs to be liberated from today is the cultural pressure to use bottles, pacifiers, and baby foods and to leave baby at home. She needs to be liberated from the hospital that "owns" the baby, from the doctor who says, "You do as I say or else," from the relatives who fear she will starve the baby, and from a society that promotes working mothers and child-care centers, thus pressuring women to work even when it is not a financial necessity. She needs to be liberated from any pressure that contradicts her natural mothering role. What she truly needs is support from the hospital, doctor, relatives, and society.

Liberation via the bottle truly ties a mother down to gadgets and to the expectations of others that she should use whatever technology has made available. The liberation that we should be striving for today is natural mothering, that type of baby care which offers the woman advantages, including the personal satisfaction that a woman can experience only through breast-feeding and the total giving of herself to her baby. It's the type of mothering a woman doesn't want to delegate to another person. It's the type of mothering that gives her a deep feeling of pride in her motherly accomplishments and that may still permeate her attitudes even after her breast-feeding days are over.

Take, for example, the problem of the tired child having difficulty going to sleep. I have known mothers who used strict words, physical threats, candy bars, and even aspirins to get their child to sleep. Yet the natural approach is so much easier—the giving of self in time by lying with the child, rubbing his back, rocking him, singing a soft, slow song, and so on. This approach gives the mother a sense of well-being, since she knows that her personal efforts and care helped soothe her child into a deep sleep. The mother who breast-feeds is, I would think, more inclined to give of herself later as she did in earlier days.

Since we're speaking of quality of life, I would like also to emphasize that much of the richness and happiness in life comes from giving. Too many women today are too concerned about their careers or outside accomplishments at the expense of their husbands, families, the unborn, and the young baby or child. Personal fulfillment is the goal. With breast-feeding, however, I feel that a woman learns that true fulfillment comes in the giving and not the taking. Being human, we know that we have to work at developing certain virtues; no one is naturally good or loving. We think of ourselves or we lose patience with others. It is a continual job to put ourselves at the service of others and to develop better traits. With breast-feeding it might be said that the maturity and character development of the mother can be formed in a very gradual and easy manner. Breast-feeding and natural mothering provide a key means whereby the mother learns to think of others—in this sense her children—and to develop certain virtues that will aid her during her entire mothering career.

POLLUTION

The environmentalists should take an interest in advocating breast-feeding, since it does not contribute to the pollution of our air or water, nor does it detract from the environment. Bottle-

74

feeding does involve the throwing away of certain items such as bottles, bottle liners, nipples, pacifiers, baby jars, cereal boxes, sterilizers, formula cans, bottle brushes, and so forth. In addition, bottle-feeding entails the use of electricity, gas, or detergent water in the preparing, heating, or sterilizing of the milk or food and the cleansing of the equipment to be used.

In our affluent society, we commonly observe the discarding of good clothes. Clothes that could be mended with a good patch or new zipper are simply thrown in the trash. With bottle-feeding, a considerable number of good baby clothes and plastic bibs are likely to be discarded during the early months after childbirth. Juices stain baby clothes so that they are soon unpresentable and are therefore, although still not worn, discarded. With a breast-fed baby, no clothes are stained. You can dress your baby up for a special occasion without worrying about food stains ruining the outfit. Another mother claimed it's ecologically best for mother's clothes, too; she noted that her bottle babies ruined her good clothes when they spit up milk, whereas her breast babies' milk wiped off easily without leaving an odor. She enjoyed not having to wash or dry clean her clothes as frequently as in the past.

With natural breast-feeding there would also be some decrease in the usage of sanitary napkins, since mothers would be averaging over a year without menstruating after childbirth. Likewise, there would be a decrease in sales of bottle-related items, which would lower their production and thus decrease the amount of pollution connected with such production. There is no doubt that natural breast-feeding could have a favorable impact toward a better tomorrow from an environmental standpoint.

Unfortunately much attention has been drawn to the fact that DDT has been found in some mother's milk, thus implying that bottle-feeding is the best alternative. However, many doctors feel strongly that the baby may be exposed to a greater concentration of DDT if he is taken off the breast and exposed directly to milks and other foods contaminated with DDT. The press failed to report that the Swedish scientist Dr. Loforth, who was the first to state publicly that DDT was in mother's milk, also pointed out emphatically that the advantages of breast milk far outweighed this negative factor. Other medical reports, as well as an ecological center in California, came out with this same conclusion: the presence of DDT in mother's milk at present levels will not cause any harm to the baby.[9] The real answer to this problem is to fight food pollution. As one mother said, "Let's get DDT out of our foods, but not breast milk out of our babies."

Other couples carry their interest in ecological breast-feeding to the wider area of natural family planning. One nursing mother who identified herself as not being affiliated with any religious group wrote as follows:

The reason that I am greatly enthused about natural family planning, and will use it to the exclusion of any artificial method of contraception, is not because of religious or moral reasons, but because of health reasons. Artificial contraception is yet another way of pollution. It pollutes the body just as our city water and air, the many additives in our foods and bottle-feeding do. You are aware of the fact that with the ecology movement more and more people are becoming interested in antipolluting ways of living in every form possible. Birth control will be no exception. Let's hope that eventually natural family planning will be used by all those interested in keeping themselves, and the future generations, as pure as possible.

POPULATION

No one needs this book to acquaint herself with the population problems in various places throughout the world. However, more attention needs to be given to the role that ecological breast-feeding can play in the birthrate. The decline in breast-feeding should be seen as an important factor in the increased birthrates among some of the developing peoples of the world, and the presence of long-term ecological breast-feeding must be recognized as a key factor in the low birthrates of some primitive peoples.

A neighbor, upon watching a TV special on the Tasadays in the Philippines, was anxious to come over and tell me how long they breast-fed their children and how the research people were amazed at their low birthrate. She, of course, immediately suspected that breast-feeding played a big factor in the low birthrate, as the

9. Interested persons can obtain information about the DDT content in breast milk from La Leche League International (see pages 97–98).

children are nursed into their early childhood. These were the same people referred to earlier in this chapter as having an absence of violence in their lives.

A Canadian research doctor has expressed concern about the relationship between breast-feeding and the population explosion of some countries. Dr. Otto Schaefer claims that prolonged lactation of about three years among the Eskimos kept the family size small, and that the availability of bottles and milk condensates to the Eskimos via trading posts changed the fertility patterns immensely. Dr. Schaefer wrote of his finding in the journal *Nutrition Today*:

As something of a diversion while I was in Baffin Island in the mid-1950's, I made calculations that indicated that the intervals between siblings shrank in direct relation to the mileage of the family from the trading posts. The shorter the distance, the more frequently they had children. The effect of rapid development of communications and the consequent movement of former camp Eskimos into large settlements is reflected in the more than 50 percent jump in the Eskimo birthrate in the Northwest Territories alone, and the increase from less than 40 births per 1000 in the mid-1950's to 64 per 1000 ten years later. In fact, it is seldom realized that in the last 20 years the Eskimos' population explosion has been as great as or greater than that which has occurred in any developing nation in the world. This is due less to the reduction in infant mortality than to the jump in birthrate. And it is far more intense for the urbanized Eskimo than for those who still live in the scattered hunting camps. There is a clear relationship between the increasing use of bottle feeding and the shortening of lactation. This important point is usually overlooked in searches for explanations of the population explosion seen in developing countries.[10]

Natural mothering isn't going to cure all of the problems of the world, but it does have some far-reaching effects. At the family level, it contributes to the physical and emotional health of both mother and baby. At the larger community level, it results in less pollution in a number of ways, and, at the level of both the individual family and the world, it provides a natural form of birth regulation. With all this going for natural mothering, it would seem more than appropriate that it be encouraged at every level.

10. *Op. cit.,* p. 16.

8

Getting Off to a Good Start

The most successful breast-feeding and natural mothering experiences are those that get off to a good start. This is not to say that mothers who have gotten off to a poor start cannot have rewarding mothering experiences, but it is obvious that it is more pleasant to have everything going for you from the beginning than to experience all sorts of problems.

There are various factors involved in getting off to a good start. Some have to do with the mental and physical preparation of the mother; others have to do with her doctor, her childbirth experience, the hospital care after delivery, and her advisers, whether freely chosen or self-appointed. Sometimes all of these favorably combine for a delightful experience; at other times a mother may have to be very determined and even courageous in order to arrange to have things working for her instead of against her.

THE MOTHER HERSELF

In conversations about the desirability of breast-feeding and its naturalness, the first question that usually arises is, "What about the mother who can't nurse?" First of all, I want to make it clear that I admit that some women can't breast-feed, but in the same breath I want to make it equally clear that I think that those who are physically unable to breast-feed are about as rare as those who are physically unable to swim. A mother who has had both breasts surgically removed would obviously be physically unable to nurse her baby, just as a person without arms or legs would be unable to swim. Also, a woman taking an oral contraceptive *should not* nurse, because it may adversely affect the baby; furthermore, the "pill" tends to suppress lactation. However, the vast majority of those mothers who "can't nurse" are in the same category as those who "can't swim"—they have never learned how.

"Doesn't this contradict all that you said about the naturalness of breast-feeding?" is another typical question. Without getting into a long debate about what is natural to man, I think that a couple of examples can help to clarify the matter. Most of us would agree that it is the most natural thing in the world for a child of seven or eight to walk on two feet and to talk. Yet this is something that the young child has to learn from his society. The study of the few so-called "nature children" has found that these children, reared by animals apart from man, were unable to speak when first discovered and learned to talk only with great difficulty later on. Two children reported to have been nursed and reared by a she-wolf when found by men were walking on all fours at the age of about seven or eight. It seems evident that, aside from a few instinctive actions such as sucking and crying, almost everything else we take for granted as natural to man has to be learned from human society. So it is with swimming and with breast-feeding. If society looked down on the idea of girls swimming, we would have very few women swimmers. If society looks down on or at least does not encourage breast-feeding, we are going to have few women successfully breast-feeding.

There are many reasons given by mothers as to why they were unable to nurse. They had the desire, but they say: "I did not have enough milk," "My milk was too watery," "My nipples were too sore," "I have an inverted nipple," "I had an abscess," "My doctor told me to quit," and so forth. However, the real reason why these mothers did not nurse was probably their lack of information and the lack of proper advice and encouragement from someone who was familiar with this natural process.

Whether a mother nurses or not—or at least whether she gets off to a good start—may be influenced largely by the type of childbirth experience she has had or by the hospital policies that she had to abide by. For example, a mother may not have enough milk because she is severely restricted from nursing her baby at the hospital where she is staying. Maybe she and thus her baby were overmedicated during the birth experience, so that the baby's sucking response was very poor. Maybe the hospital is giving her baby sugared water or formula in the nursery, and thus she is given a sleepy, full baby at feeding times. Perhaps the hospital has taught the baby to prefer the rubber nipple by offering bottles and pacifiers in the nursery. And, as the mother left the hospital, maybe she was handed a pack of free formula, a gift that might encourage her to use bottles when her milk supply is low instead of simply increasing the nursings. Unfortunately, the use of bottles will dry up her supply even more. Sad but true, most hospitals do not offer the nursing mother proper support. Instead they promote policies and practices that are obstacles to any successful nursing program.

Breast problems such as abscesses, engorgement, or plugged ducts would be reduced in frequency if hospitals allowed mothers to nurse their babies as often and as much as the baby desired and if mothers were educated to desire this type of unrestricted nursing. Using the excuse that it will make more milk, some hospital nurses do not allow mothers to express themselves when their breasts are painfully full. Our concern, however, is not the production of more milk but the elimination of the engorgement or the excess milk to avoid the future development of abscesses or plugged ducts and, in addition, to offer the mother immediate relief by such expression. In 1968 I was greatly surprised to be bound tightly around the chest area immediately after the birth of our third child. The reason given was that this would offer support like a bra even for the nursing mother. Tightness around the breasts can lead to breast problems, so I removed this binding as soon as I left the delivery room. Certainly no mother could nurse her baby with such a contraption wrapped around her.

As for sore nipples, this problem can be partially reduced or eliminated by preparing or toughening the nipple area prior to childbirth. The nipples can be lightly rubbed with a plain wet washcloth at bathing time or a soft dry cloth or towel any time during the day.

I truly sympathize with those women who have experienced

sore, cracked, or bleeding nipples. Having been too lazy to practice what I preach, I have experienced the distinct discomfort of nursing with sore and cracked nipples. With adequate care I was able to eliminate the soreness in about two weeks' time, but many mothers do not know how to care for sore nipples properly. In such a situation the nipples can become worse and actually bleed, causing the mother to seek relief through bottle-feeding. Or the mother will be determined to continue the nursing and suffer through six weeks of sore nipples when maybe with proper care she could have healed the nipples much faster. It does help to know that this soreness will eventually go away and that there are things you can do to help yourself in this particular situation.

For one thing, you need not restrict nursing with sore nipples. The discomfort associated with sore nipples is usually experienced right at the beginning of the feeding. Once the milk starts to flow the pain subsides, and you will be able to nurse with little discomfort; thus you may let your baby nurse for a long time without removing him from the breast.

Indeed, with most breast problems you will usually want to nurse the baby for as long as he desires at one feeding. The best therapy for a plugged duct or a breast abscess is to allow the baby to nurse as often and as long as possible on the affected breast in order to keep the breast empty. Hand expression is also an additional help. The worst thing you can do at this time is to leave the breast alone. Unfortunately and unnecessarily, some doctors recommend abrupt weaning or cessation of nursing on the infected breast.

Women may complain about inverted nipples, but a truly inverted nipple is very uncommon. If a mother does have such a nipple, she can wear a special shield[1] that will tend to draw the nipple out.

Several couples have told us that they had to quit nursing because their baby had diarrhea. They have been misinformed. A doctor friend who is well read on the breast-fed baby says that a baby does not have to be taken off the breast for any type of diarrhea unless the baby is so sick that he needs transfusions and couldn't nurse anyway. It is, in fact, the other way around. One

1. Available through La Leche League.

mother told me that when her baby had severe diarrhea, her doctor advised total breast-feeding. Later, when the crisis was past, he told her she would have lost the baby if she had not been nursing. What some mothers or their doctor understand to be diarrhea is sometimes just the soft liquid stool of a breast-fed baby. This stool will remain a thick liquid up until the time the child begins solids. A baby was not meant to have a hard-formed stool. In addition, in the early days a baby may have several movements a day or a spotting with each feeding.

Later, couples begin to worry about the opposite: they fear the baby is constipated. As the baby gets older, he may at times have a bowel movement once every two or three days. There may be a few times when he will go even seven days without a bowel movement, but the stool is very soft when it arrives—and that is the important point. If a mother realizes that breast milk is utilized very efficiently by the baby's body and that little is eliminated as waste products, she can understand why it might take several days for her baby to build up enough of a supply of waste matter before there is adequate pressure for elimination.

There are also many situations in which a doctor will tell the mother to quit nursing altogether or to quit nursing for a given period of time, such as one week or one month. It is extremely rare that a mother would have to quit nursing, and any such recommendation can be met with "But doctor, I don't want to quit." If he sees that nursing means so much to you, he is more likely to appreciate any possible alternative.[2] Most likely, you will learn that nursing can be continued. However, if the doctor is not willing to offer you support, then try to find one who will.

It goes without saying that any nursing problem is more difficult to take care of if one is beset with lots of company. It's hard enough finding time to follow instructions given by a counseling mother without worrying about entertaining people.

My intention here is not to provide a series of handy solutions for various breast-feeding problems. My main purpose is to show that most reasons given for cessation of nursing are not valid. Any mother who is experiencing difficulty or has questions

2. Contact the Professional Advisory Board of La Leche League International (see list of addresses facing p. 1) for advice and information.

with regard to nursing should contact a local La Leche League group. It is interesting to note from my mail that most of the mothers who write are most appreciative for the help and information they received from this organization, which is dedicated to helping mothers nurse their babies. Having the right answer and support at the right time can mean success instead of failure.

I believe that almost any woman can learn this natural art well if she really has the desire. Her learning process should start during the months before childbirth so that she is well prepared for her hospital stay and the early weeks at home. She should learn what she can do physically to prepare herself, and, of equal importance, she and her husband should become psychologically prepared to meet the possible objections of well-meaning but misinformed or uninformed persons ranging from the doctor or hospital nurse to friends and relatives. On the subject of breast-feeding, all too many people who have never read a book or who have never nursed feel qualified to pass on advice. On the other hand, the La Leche League has a professional board of medical advisers, plus the experience of thousands of women.

Many young mothers today also lack confidence in themselves. Some have called me after they are home from the hospital to express a general feeling that everything is wrong. In the beginning of the conversation I begin to wonder if I can be of any help at all, but then soon realize that there really is no problem. Toward the end of the conversation I begin to see a completely different picture of a mother who is doing a fine job and who has a good baby, and I tell her so. These mothers only require a little more time to develop the self-confidence they need—and which should have been formed during their hospital stay, beginning at the birth of the child. It takes a little while for a first-time nursing mother to forget about rules and time schedules, and until this happens the mother does not really relax and enjoy her baby's own schedule. At any rate, all that most of these mothers need is a lot of praise, and someone telling them that they are doing what is best for their baby.

For those few mothers who may not be able to nurse their child, much of the motherly advice in this book can still be followed. The philosophy of giving of yourself, being close and in touch with your child, taking him with you as much as possible, holding him for the bottle-feedings and enjoying and loving him are the best "gifts" you can give your small child. A bottle-feeding mother can be a good mother, and there is no guarantee that breast-feeding always produces a good mother. However if everything else is equal, it's just easier to practice good mothering the natural way of breast-feeding.

THE DOCTOR

This is a most delicate subject, for three reasons. In the eyes of many a woman, her doctor occupies the only pedestal of infallibility remaining in modern life. She knows her husband makes mistakes; the newspapers won't let her forget that politicians make mistakes. Thus, of the old idols of everyday life, only the doctor remains on his pedestal, thanks to the new reverence for science. Secondly, because doctors are so very human, it is possible that even a moderate objectively critical word about medical practices may alienate some of them from the very positive values of fostering the natural processes. Thirdly, any criticism of medical practitioners "in general" will not be universally valid because there are many wonderful exceptions who are currently encouraging mothers in the natural art of breast-feeding.

I think it is being very safe and conservative to say that in what follows I am merely echoing what some members of the medical profession have already said in medical journals, in magazines, in convention proceedings, and in private conversations about the attitudes of their own profession with respect to breast-feeding.

The problem is that breast-feeding is not a disease but a normal and healthy practice; and for this reason all too many doctors know all too little about it. It is too natural a process to have occupied much place in their medical training. That is, the traditional medical school has been oriented toward preparing doctors to diagnose disease. In the limited time available, attention has been focused on the pathological condition rather than on the fostering of the natural, healthy condition.

The medical student will learn about various things that can go wrong with the breast, such as a breast abscess or a breast cancer. He may study briefly, if at all, the care of the normal, healthy baby through breast-feeding. With regard to the baby, he will probably learn the various illnesses and allergies and how to diagnose and remedy them. He will learn about formulas, and will imbibe his professor's theories about introducing solid foods to the bottle-fed baby.

Since he is not familiar with the natural plan for feeding babies, the doctor is not equipped to offer the necessary advice that a nursing mother needs. He finds, therefore, that it is much easier to recommend the bottle when a nursing mother comes to him for advice.

The doctor is also a man of his culture. In a society in which breast-feeding has become less and less popular, it is quite likely that his wife did not nurse or did not nurse for any length of time. She probably went to the formulas or to "what the doctor prescribed." I wonder, too, if it wouldn't be hard for a doctor to recommend breast-feeding to his patients when he might not have recommended it for his own wife and children. Thus we are faced with a situation whereby some doctors may advise their patients not on the basis of medical research and the experience of successful nursing mothers, but rather on the basis of his own family and practice.

What is the role of the physician in breast-feeding? Certainly, his influence is considerable with most mothers. Many mothers look to their doctors for approval; some will not nurse their babies without the doctor's permission! He is therefore in an excellent position to foster the practice of breast-feeding and natural mothering. He can explain to the mother how her milk is the best food for the baby; he can tell her all the health advantages to both the baby and to herself through breast-feeding; he can tell her about natural mothering and the natural infertility of ecological breast-feeding. He can assure her that she will be able to do a good job; he might recommend attending La Leche League meetings during pregnancy. He can tell her how much money she will save by not using bottles, formulas, and baby foods, and he might even tell her that it would be worthwhile for her to spend some of her savings to buy this book!

Unfortunately, many doctors do not offer the support that a mother needs, or may give only partial approval by implying that it's something they will go along with since it means so much to the mother. However, many mothers choose to remain with their doctor unless he is too upset about the breast-feeding. Many doctors do look upon breast-feeding as a "kooky" exception instead of the natural norm. They will also discredit any relationship between proper breast-feeding and infertility or the benefits of natural childbirth or the reliability of natural family planning. In a way, these doctors are more to be pitied than blamed, because their whole training has been in terms of drugs and devices, with no orientation toward fostering the natural. Still, as men of science, they are supposed to have open minds.

THE CHILDBIRTH EXPERIENCE

Another way in which a doctor can be either most helpful or most uncooperative for the prospective nursing mother is in the process of childbirth itself. Under healthy, normal, natural conditions, a new baby should be nursing within a few minutes after childbirth. This is just as much for the mother's benefit as for his, because his sucking helps her uterus to contract and thus shut off maternal blood vessels that formerly took care of him. In brief, that means that his sucking helps to prevent hemorrhaging in his mother.[3] His continued sucking in the next 24 to 48 hours gives him the benefits of a fluid called *colostrum* while it continues to put her uterus back into shape. Colostrum is the name given to the first milk secreted by the breast; it is much richer and creamier than the milk that soon follows (and which, by the way, may look thinner than the milk you would buy in the store, an appearance that does not, however, discredit its value).

I cannot emphasize too strongly that a mother should allow her baby to breast-feed without restriction during the first twenty-four hours after delivery. There is evidence that the baby's sucking reflex "is at its height twenty to thirty minutes after birth. If the infant is not fed, then the reflex diminishes rapidly and reappears forty hours

3. Robert Bradley, *Husband-Coached Childbirth* (New York: Harper & Row, 1965), pp. 75–76.

later."[4] If you want a successful nursing experience, start early. Don't be surprised if your baby doesn't nurse a minute or so after his birth. He will do better a few minutes later. At a minimum, your baby should be allowed to nurse within the first half-hour after birth and at least every three hours in the next twenty-four.

The reason I want to be emphatic on this early nursing is because many women do not succeed in nursing their babies, and a major cause is the failure to get off to a good start in the hospital. On the other hand, some doctors see no nursing failures because they have given their patients the proper advice for those critical first days of nursing. Dr. Richard Applebaum, a Miami pediatrician, likes to have a *pre*natal visit with the prospective mother to explain some of the basic physiology of lactation. He stresses the importance of frequent nursing in that first twenty-four-hour period, as well as later, in order to avoid engorgement when the milk starts coming in larger quantities. He also tells a mother to make sure that her obstetrician leaves orders at the hospital that the baby is not to have a rubber nipple in his mouth.[5] In his *Abreast of the Times*,[6] Dr. Applebaum uses illustrations to show the difference in the baby's tongue action with the breast as opposed to the rubber nipple. If a baby becomes accustomed to the rubber nipple, he may have great difficulty in adjusting to his mother's breast. Dr. Applebaum also strongly discourages bringing any formula home from the hospital because its very presence can lead the new mother to lose confidence.

In order for mother and baby to have this good start at nursing, they both have to be physically able right after the birth. Thus I recommend a prepared, natural, and—if possible—completely unmedicated childbirth as the best start for a successful breast-feeding experience. A mother who is unconscious from anesthesia cannot

4. "Together, and Nursing, from Birth," La Leche League International Information Sheet no. 20 (January 1978). This sheet referred to research by I. A. Archavsky, "Immediate Breast-feeding of Newborn Infant in the Prophylaxis of the So-Called Physiological Loss of Weight" (text in Russian), *Vopr. Pediatri*. 20 (1952): 45-53. Abstract in *Courier* 3 (1953): 170.

5. La Leche League International, Transcripts of Third Biennial Convention at Denver, 1968, pp. 127-129 (no longer available).

6. 1969. Available through LLLI and ICEA (see list of addresses facing p. 1).

breast-feed. Just as importantly, her baby may have been adversely affected by the anesthetic used on her. Respiratory distress in the newborn has long been known to be caused by obstetrical medication. Furthermore, "sedatives containing barbiturates administered to the mother during labor have been shown to adversely affect the infant's sucking reflexes for 4 to 5 days after birth."[7]

Although the regional anesthesias seem to be a big improvement over general anesthesia, health hazards to the newborn may still exist. The spinal anesthesias may result in a drop in maternal blood pressure, thus adversely affecting circulation in the uterus; and this circulation may remain impaired.[8] Apparently, the maternal anesthetic that is the safest for the unborn child is the pudendal block, which is administered only into the tissues surrounding the birth canal. None of the spinal anesthesias make it impossible to breast-feed immediately after childbirth, but the pudendal would seem to be the least departure from a totally natural and unmedicated delivery.

To get off to the best start for successful nursing, a mother should begin nursing right on the delivery table with an alert, undrugged baby. That in turn means she has to have a physician who will, first of all, allow her to nurse after childbirth and who will also assist the delivery in such a way as to leave both her and the baby *able* to nurse. The next thing she normally needs from her physician is the *absence* of a shot to contract her uterus: baby's sucking takes care of that. Then she needs the *absence* of any kind of a shot to dry up her milk supply. None of this seems to be asking very much, but a mother may have to shop around before finding a doctor who will be agreeable.

THE BABY'S DOCTOR

Finding a child's doctor who is favorable to total breast-feeding may be another problem. Lucky is the woman who has found a family-practice doctor who takes care of both mother and baby

7. Doris Haire, "The Cultural Warping of Childbirth," *ICEA News,* Spring 1972, p. 10. Mrs. Haire in this well-documented report offers the following references for the above quotation: T. B. Brazelton, "Effect of Maternal Medication on the Neonate and his Behavior," *Journal of Pediatrics* 58 (1961): 513–518, R. Kron, "Newborn Sucking Behavior Affected by Obstetric Sedation," *Pediatrics* 37 (1966): 1012–1016.
8. *Ibid.*

from birth on. Many women will be using specialists for both obstetrics and pediatrics, thus doubling their potential doctor shopping. Sometimes it's possible to find a pediatrician who is well-informed about breast-feeding and who will support you all the way. At other times you may have to compromise and go to a doctor who disapproves but will continue to see your baby. If you already have a relationship of long standing with a particular doctor, you may want to stay with him even if he's not an advocate of breast-feeding. If he knows you, he may be quite interested in your new ideas, and quite receptive to your complete breast-feeding. One mother recently expressed concern as to what her doctor's reaction might be to complete breast-feeding, since he had put her previous babies on solids within several weeks after birth. She later told me that he went along with her although he mentioned solids at each visit. But he jokingly told her, "You know more about it than I." Such a doctor may be more open to a mother he already has a good relationship with than he might be to a total stranger.

On the other hand, there are still a great number of physicians whose habit of recommending early solids and liquid supplements is very strong. If your doctor should be one of those who recommends solids or juice soon after birth, you might ask him why breast milk isn't sufficient. Many doctors will go along with the mother if she expresses her feelings on the matter in a gentle, sincere manner. Mothers also find it helpful to have their husbands present for moral support. If your doctor should be particularly insistent, you may choose several alternatives. You might ask him for the research that backs up his apparent contention that the normal mother's milk alone in the early months isn't sufficient. Since there isn't any such research, you may be putting him in a very defensive position. Perhaps a more diplomatic way might be to say that you understand that there has been considerable research supporting the idea that total breast-feeding for the first six months is the best nutrition and that anemia is rare in the breast-fed baby. You might want to have in your purse a copy of the La Leche League research leaflet titled *Anemia: Rare in Breastfed Babies*.[9] Some mothers choose to handle it one month at a time by saying, "The baby is doing so well, doctor—wouldn't it

9. Available from La Leche League (see list of addresses facing p. 1).

be possible to continue this way a while longer?" Others who have the strength of their convictions just ignore the doctor's advice, relying on his compliments about the health of the baby at the regular visits as confirmation of their baby care through total breast-feeding. Still others will simply change doctors.

THE HOSPITAL

Hospitals provide the first environment for the vast majority of newborn babies and their mothers. The official policies of the institutions and the personal attitudes of the nurses can have a significant influence on the success of breast-feeding. Each of these sources can be helpful; yet it is the unfortunate fact that too frequently they are either of no help or are actively detrimental.

I really don't have too many nice things to say about hospitals with regard to childbirth procedures or infant care. There is a slow trend to accommodate those couples who desire the natural approach in childbirth and in breast-feeding, but these changes have not yet occurred at many hospitals. My best advice is to choose the hospital that will offer you the most support. My next advice is to leave as early as possible. If you had a medicated delivery, then wait until the effects of the drug have worn off and until you are feeling well.

Such advice undoubtedly raises a few eyebrows. Whenever I and my husband tell people that with our last two babies I came home within six hours after delivery, we receive looks of utter disbelief. In both cases in two different cities, I was apparently the first such patient for each doctor, but there was no problem. My husband and I had simply talked about this with the doctor during my prenatal visits and requested that I be allowed to go home a few hours after delivery if everything was medically satisfactory with both me and the baby. By showing my willingness to stay in the hospital if either my baby or I really needed its special care facilities, I put the doctor at ease; on the other hand, he would have to have some medically valid reason (for example, something wrong with either me or the baby) in order to keep us in the hospital. In each case, both the baby and and I were medically in good shape, so we went home where we could get adequate rest.

Such ideas didn't originate with me. Rather, I was heavily influenced by the writings of two doctors who have related their experiences with such practices and secondly by mothers who chose to have home deliveries in order to avoid any hospital interference. Dr. Robert Bradley, in *Husband-Coached Childbirth*,[10] relates how normal women in his practice return home within several hours after childbirth. I was impressed also by the way in which Dr. Morris Gold,[11] of Lynnwood, Washington, gradually became aware that it was perfectly compatible with good health care for normal mothers and their newborn babies to return home a few hours after delivery. Of course, both of these doctors provided their patients with proper and supportive prenatal training and an environment during labor and delivery that is conducive toward the unmedicated delivery.

All too many hospitals routinely offend against the mother-baby ecology. They separate mother and baby right at birth. They will place baby in a boxlike warming device instead of wrapping him in mother's arms. They will not allow you to nurse the baby until twelve or even twenty-four hours after childbirth. They will encourage the use of bottles and sugared water. They will remind you of the free formula pack you can take home with you. Nursing is restricted, and orders to bring the baby to you when hungry and *not* to give the baby supplements in the nursery—which has been found to be a good place for a baby to pick up an infection—are frequently ignored.

Indeed, hospitals are good places to have a baby—providing

10. New York: Harper & Row, 1965.
11. Paper presented at the Third Biennial Convention of the La Leche League International, 1968.

there is support for natural childbirth—but bad places to leave a healthy baby. Dr. Herbert Ratner, a public health director, when speaking before a medical convention, stated that for the optimum health of the infant, well-born babies should be discharged from the hospital having had nothing except mother's milk.[12] Unfortunately, the breast-fed baby who has had nothing but mother's milk at the hospital is rare.

The hospital environment can play a crucial role in helping or hindering the nursing couple. As I have stressed throughout this book, the only schedule in natural breast-feeding is the baby's. Thus the hospital atmosphere conducive to breast-feeding will be the one that allows the mother and baby to remain together as much as possible.

Rooming-in presents the best alternative to going home within a few hours after birth. If such a program isn't available, a policy of bringing the baby to the mother or of allowing the mother to go to the baby to nurse in a special room off the nursery for all feedings is the next best thing. The breast-feeding baby will benefit from the rich colostrum, and will have a nice soft nipple for easy learning until his mother's milk comes in. His frequent nursing will help to relieve or minimize the engorgement that frequently results from the unnatural separation of mother and baby.

Many mothers quit nursing within the first few weeks because rooming-in facilities or adequate alternatives were not available. During his individual hospital stay, the baby is learning to suck on rubber nipples in the nursery, and as a result he may nurse only occasionally when he is fortunate enough to visit his mother. The learning process of natural breast-feeding therefore has to be postponed until the nursing couple go home. Then they are lucky if they have the time to learn together and to adjust to the new change before friends and relatives start visiting. It requires more time and effort on the part of the mother to persevere and to learn what she should have learned, in an easier way, right from childbirth.

Many maternity wards are administered under a hotel policy.

12. Herbert Ratner, "The Public Health Aspects of Breast-feeding" (Paper read at the AMA, 107th Annual Meeting, San Francisco, 1958), La Leche League Reprint no. 52, (Franklin Park, Ill., 1971).

"You're here for a little rest so don't worry about your baby. We'll take care of him for you. You'll have plenty of time for that when you get home." Some doctors will discourage rooming-in because they equate it with diaper changing. "You'll have plenty of diapers to change when you go home," or "Why not take a rest while you can?" All of these views neglect the reality that the mother has a very special job to do in fulfilling the needs of her baby. There is more to baby care than work and changing diapers, and there is more to mothering than giving birth or figuring out how to get away from it all. Mothering instead should be more centered around the nutritional, emotional, and physical needs of the baby, and this could be put into practice on the hospital level as well.

There is research to indicate that a mother's "mothering instinct" is inhibited by the traditional American hospital routine that separates mother and baby. In fact, while the first twenty-four hours seem to be especially important in establishing normal mother-baby relationships,[13] this is the time when normal hospital routine allows for minimal contact between mother and baby.

Many hospitals are now asking patients for an evaluation of their services. Whether it is asked for or not, it would be helpful to write the hospital complimenting them on their good points but also expressing your interests in other services you hope they will have in the near future. It is amazing how fast hospital policies can change in a short period of time; the hospital can be very receptive to what the consumer wants, and, with the declining birthrate and inflationary costs, they have additional reasons to listen.

Perhaps a few reflections on my own experiences can illustrate some of the things a mother may encounter by way of doctors and hospitals. Because our family has been one of those mobile ones you read about in the statistics, I have had a variety of experiences. We have had a different doctor for each of our four children. Our first doctor discouraged the natural-spacing effects of breast-feeding, and he was highly critical of the available natural childbirth classes in the area. I went to the classes anyway, and was extremely grateful for having done so. It was also at these classes that I was introduced to La Leche League, an organization that made a good impact on our family.

13. *Ibid.,* pp. 27, 28.

Our second doctor encouraged the total breast-feeding rule for family-planning purposes, but he discouraged rooming-in and husbands in the delivery room. He did leave orders that our baby was not to receive supplements in the nursery room. These orders were apparently followed. However, I still wanted to try the other system so I switched to rooming-in, before going home, and found it a great improvement.

With our third child on the way we found out that our doctor wanted to routinely catheterize me before and after delivery and insisted upon a shot to contract my uterus even with immediate breast-feeding. Fortunately I had had prior experience with two cooperative obstetricians before encountering this anesthesiologist-turned-general-practitioner, and neither of the first two had made such suggestions. This third doctor, up to the time of this, my eighth month of pregnancy, had been very cooperative, but now he turned tough, perhaps thinking that he could do as he pleased with me at this stage of the game. With my husband's support I terminated the relationship at that point, and found another doctor who was cooperative.

With our last two babies, I asked the doctors to let me go home a few hours after childbirth, and both agreed I could. My husband was also allowed to observe the birth of our fourth child. With this last baby, alertness paid off. I was taking care of the baby on the delivery table when out of the corner of my eye I saw the nurse approach me from behind with a long needle in her hand. I immediately asked her what it was for, and she said it was to contract the uterus. I told her I never had it with my other three babies, and the doctor then told her I didn't need it. Obstetrical medication is *so* routine that even when you have the best of natural childbirth doctors, you still have to be alert about the hospital personnel.

From my personal experiences, I can draw several lessons that may have wide applicability in helping mothers get off to a good start in breast-feeding and natural mothering.

1. Express your feelings to the doctor and explain why you feel the way you do. Don't come armed with literature as if you expect a fight. Read any available literature yourself to become better informed and to be able to express yourself better when conversing

94

with your doctor. If you feel the doctor may not be agreeable, have your husband come with you for support.

2. Remember that you have the right to be selective in choosing your obstetrician, pediatrician, or family doctor. Exercise this right. Ask questions plainly. Having a list of important questions helps you to remember the things you wanted to ask. If a doctor has a set way of doing things, don't be afraid to ask why. You have a right to refuse unnecessary treatment.

3. Be specific. Ask ahead of time whether you can have your baby with you after childbirth, whether you can have an unmedicated childbirth experience or at least a minimal amount of drugs if needed, whether you can totally nurse the baby for the first six months, and so forth.

4. You have a right to your own baby. He does not belong to the hospital.

5. You have a right to leave the hospital as soon as it is possible, consistent with your health and that of the baby.

6. You have a right to have the natural care that is best for you and your baby. And you can feel secure knowing that "science" is there for the unusual circumstance should you or the baby require special treatment.

7. Since "natural" in man does not mean the same as "automatic," you have a corresponding duty to prepare yourself ahead of time both intellectually and physically in order to fully assist the natural processes. Don't expect a natural-type childbirth experience without childbirth preparation. And don't expect a successful nursing experience without learning something about breast-feeding. Make use of the services provided by childbirth education groups and by La Leche League and other nursing-mother groups.

8. Learn with your husband whenever possible. Share with him anything new that you've learned through contact with other nursing mothers or through reading.

9. You have a right to terminate your relationship with your doctor. If he won't go along with the best in maternal or pediatric care, don't feel you are obliged to stay with him.

10. If you move into a new area, there are several ways to look for a doctor or groups who promote the natural approach: (a)

Contact the local newspapers, especially reporters for the women's or family section of the paper. They should be able to tell you if there are La Leche League meetings or childbirth classes in the area. If there is a doctor in the area who is noted for encouraging natural childbirth, breast-feeding, or family-centered maternity care, then most likely a reporter has done a write-up on him. (b) Look in the phone book for a listing of La Leche League or call the local hospitals; a nurse on the maternity floor may be able to help you locate such groups, which will possibly be able to give you several references with regard to doctors. (c) Call various doctors' offices and ask the nurse or receptionist questions to determine if the doctor is in favor of the natural approach. She will most likely have the doctor return your call at a convenient time. If he is not interested, he may know of a doctor who is. Take as much care in shopping for a doctor as you would in shopping for an automobile.

If you know that breast-feeding is best for your baby; if you know that a good start is important in the breast-feeding–natural mothering relationship; if you know that obstetrical medication may have certain hazards for your baby and may impede early breast-feeding, then it seems to me that as an informed couple you would want to do everything reasonably possible to insure that the doctor, the hospital, and the childbirth experience will work together in getting the breast-feeding off to a good start. Sometimes I wonder if there isn't even some sort of an obligation to do what is naturally best for our babies, even when it means more effort on our part and a certain amount of criticism as we try to get away from cultural practices without dropping out of our society.

OTHER ADVISERS

In addition to medical doctors, a mother may seek and receive advice from other persons. She may be seeking information about family planning, about breast-feeding for its own sake, or about breast-feeding as a means of family planning. Her advisers may range from her clergyman to the mother-in-law of the gal three doors down the street. In addition to these personal forms of advice, a mother or prospective mother may seek information from various courses offered in the community. Schools, colleges, and churches offer courses on marriage and family life, and frequently they have the opportunity to touch upon baby care, parenthood, and family planning.

Prenatal classes are usually offered in many communities, and the teacher here can greatly influence her students. One class I attended during my first pregnancy encouraged mothers to nurse their babies, and everyone wanted to nurse except one. However, in a similar class in a different city four years later, breast-feeding was hardly mentioned. The instructor, a nurse, spent some time passing out nipples and bottles—so the mothers would know how to put them together!—and toward the end of the classes she handed out family-planning literature, remarking: "If you want to plan a family, don't breast-feed." In this class, only two mothers showed any interest in nursing their babies. Since the instructor never gave her students one positive reason why they should breast-feed, very few had the desire.

Clergymen are sometimes asked for guidance about family planning. It would seem that at least they should not discourage the natural plan of baby care and of baby spacing. More affirmatively, they should know enough about the natural plan to be able to describe what is involved. They and other personal advisers, if not informed, should be able to refer the mother to someone who is or else to certain available books.

Many relatives also lack the necessary information. They would be of real help if they limited their advice to the actual knowledge they possessed, but this is unfortunately not often the case. Some relatives can deter a mother from nursing her baby by their negative remarks. Such a relative should quite obviously not be around the nursing mother after childbirth. One of my closest friends failed to nurse two babies because of her mother's presence and strong opposition to breast-feeding. With her third child she politely made sure that her mother would not be staying with them during those early postpartum days—and she had no problems nursing the baby.

Various marriage and family courses provide an excellent opportunity to educate groups of people, women and men, who are open and receptive to the ideas of natural breast-feeding. It is important in this regard that proper attitudes and information about breast-feeding should not be limited to women. Men, too, should learn all the advantages of breast-feeding, as the understanding and encouragement of a husband can be a great help to the nursing mother.

In our society, if the case for breast-feeding and natural mothering were made with the same emphasis as the presentation of the use of bottles, baby foods, the pill and other forms of contraceptives, I feel that the desires of many mothers to breast-feed would remain alive. Most couples do not consider breast-feeding because they were never presented with any reasons for doing so. A good educational program could change that picture.

In short, the hospital, nurses and doctors, clergymen, relatives and teachers, schools and churches—all play a part in the decision of a mother to nurse her baby and secondly to breast-feed in such a manner that it becomes an excellent means of spacing babies and, most importantly, of caring for babies. These people and institutions can either help greatly by inducing positive attitudes and imparting factual information about this natural process or they can do the reverse.

Where does a couple go to find support and information with regard to breast-feeding? Couples who are interested in getting off to a good start can contact two international organizations that support family-centered maternity care and breast-feeding. These organizations I have made reference to before. One is La Leche League International; the other, International Childbirth Education Association.

La Leche League International

This nonprofit, nondenominational group is dedicated to helping mothers learn "the womanly art of breast-feeding"; hence, the title of their manual. Many mothers have the idea that you should contact the league only if a problem arises. On the contrary, the league can be very valuable even to the successful nursing mother. The league also supports the type of mothering described in this book.

The league is represented by over a thousand groups located

in many towns and cities throughout the United States and in other countries. They have a regular series of meetings, during which various topics are discussed. The ideal time for a woman to complete the series is during pregnancy. The league's manual, *The Womanly Art of Breastfeeding,* is one book a nursing mother should have in her possession to read and reread when necessary. The manual can be purchased by writing La Leche League International, 9616 Minneapolis Avenue, Franklin Park, Ill. 60131.

If a group is not available in your area, you may write the league at the above address for the closest available help and their free reprint packet. This information may come in handy if any problems arise or should you desire counseling at some later date. Any medical questions can be directed to the league's medical advisory board. Some of these questions are answered in the wealth of information available in their various reprints or information sheets, and these can be obtained through local groups as well. A phone call may be considered a cheap investment when one considers the benefits of breast-feeding and the unwanted expense of bottles and baby food.[14]

International Childbirth Education Association

ICEA is in its second decade of growth. Its primary purpose is to help parents achieve satisfaction during pregnancy, labor, and delivery through educational, physical, and emotional preparation. For information with regard to available childbirth classes in your area, write the ICEA Secretary, P.O. Box 5852, Milwaukee, Wis. 53220. You may also write the ICEA Supplies Center (1414 N.W. 85th Street, Seattle, Wash. 98117) for a list of their recommended books and pamphlets.

To conclude, I would like to add that many of us who have breast-fed owe a deep debt of gratitude to a particular doctor or hospital nurse who gave us the proper support and advice with regard to childbirth and breast-feeding. It must also be realized

14. For breast-feeding help, call a local nursing group or call La Leche League International at 312 455–7730, where a League mother will be ready to answer your questions.

that most hospitals and doctors practice as they do because that is what their patients want. Mothers want to start their babies on solids right off the bat; mothers want to be knocked out during the birth; mothers tend to look to science to solve all their problems. There are doctors who would like to see a change, but they, too, are faced with the difficult job of reeducating their patients as to what is best for them. We know doctors who personally recommend breast-feeding or natural childbirth only to have most women turn up their noses. They just aren't interested.

Secondly, both the childbirth and the breast-feeding experiences are interrelated. In fact, it has been shown that women who desire breast-feeding, and have easier childbirth experiences, are more likely to express physical affection toward their children. They enjoy their mothering role in its many phases.[15] Therefore, both the childbirth and early breast-feeding experience play an important part in the mother-baby ecology. If this ecology is greatly disturbed during childbirth and the immediate postpartum hours, then the breast-feeding and natural mothering relationship may be seriously hampered and even made almost impossible.

15. Niles Newton, *Maternal Emotions* (New York: Hoeber, 1955), p. 103.

9

The First Six Months

NATURE'S PRODUCT

Your milk is the best food you can give your baby. Breast milk has the calories, proteins, vitamins, water, and other essential elements needed for the baby's growth. Nature, who did a fantastic job of nurturing and developing new life within your body for nine months before birth, has likewise provided a complete nutritious food for your baby's growth after birth. As Dr. Joseph Brenneman, original editor of *Practice of Pediatrics,* stated: "Under any circumstances breast milk is so important to the young infant that one may well think of the newborn as still vitally a part of his mother, birth having changed only the manner and substance, not the continuity, of maternal nourishment."[1] The National Research Council says that

breast milk may contain inadequate amounts of various vitamins, making supplementation desirable. These facts do not nullify the fact that human milk is the food designed by Nature for the human infant, or circumvent the truth that our present knowledge has not enabled us to produce a formula for infant feeding which can be demonstrated to represent an improvement of Nature's product.[2]

1. Lee Forest Hill, "Breast-feeding and Mixed Feeding," *Practice of Pediatrics* 1 (1966): Chapter 25.
2. National Research Council. *Maternal Nutrition and Child Health,* Publication 123, Food and Nutrition Board, National Academy of Sciences–National Research Council, Washington, D.C., 1950.

From the baby's point of view, unrestricted nursing from the very beginning may be quite important for his health. The secretion that comes from a mother's breast at birth, the colostrum, is different from and richer than the milk that will soon follow, as has already been discussed. This first milk has been reported as being valuable to the infant's health, for cells present in colostrum have been known to ingest and destroy bacteria.[3] It has also been reported that no formula can duplicate the gradual changes that occur in the colostrum and milk following childbirth. Dr. Robert Jackson

has pointed out that the proportions of the constituents in human milk gradually change; the colostrum of the first day is not the same as the colostrum of the second, and then when you get into the transitional milk there is a gradual consistent change intimately related to the needs of the baby.[4]

Thus it is seen that mother's milk is best for her baby right from the very beginning. Simple glucose or water is a poor substitute for the complex and rich initial diet the baby is entitled to receive from his mother's breast.

Breast milk contains an insufficient amount of vitamin D, but apparently nature intended that both mother and baby obtain some vitamin D out of doors, since our bodies synthesize this vitamin upon exposure to sunlight. Your doctor may or may not recommend vitamin drops for your breast-fed baby. These drops will not influence the natural-spacing benefit derived from completely nursing your baby.

Breast milk contains a plentiful supply of vitamin C when the mother's diet is adequate. This is evident when you observe any analytic breakdown of breast milk and its constituents. Therefore, juices that are often recommended in the baby's early months are unnecessary for the breast-fed baby.

Some mothers are told to give their baby extra liquid or water during the hot summer months. This also proves to be unnecessary. There is a sufficient amount of water in breast milk for the baby. If anyone needs the extra water, it would be the nursing mother

3. *La Leche League News,* November–December 1968, p. 82.
4. *La Leche League News,* November–December 1972, p. 89.

herself. Therefore, for normal healthy infants nature's complete food need not be supplemented with bottles containing juices, liquids, or plain water.

It should go without saying that a nursing mother should provide herself with good nutrition. The maternal diet is important in order for the baby to derive the greatest benefit from this ecological relationship. Therefore, during the months of pregnancy and during the months of breast-feeding a mother should take special care in selecting proper foods for herself and her family.

THE NEED FOR IRON

At birth the baby has his own supply of iron, which normally lasts until the time of weaning. If you plan to nurse your baby completely for six months or thereabouts, your doctor may want to check your baby's iron supply before he reaches six months of age. The testing is very simple, and will cause little discomfort to the baby. A finger is pricked quickly to obtain a few drops of blood, which is then measured. Many doctors do not require any testing if solids are begun at about six months of age.

It is nice to know that you may still continue to totally nurse regardless of your baby's need for iron. This is due to the fact that iron is available in drop form. Thus solid foods can be postponed until the time that the baby desires them.

SOLIDS—EARLY OR LATE?

The early introduction of solids is so common today that a mother who chooses to nurse her infant as the good Lord intended is rare indeed. Friends and relatives question her choice for fear her baby will become undernourished. For many, the saying "Breast-fed is best-fed" seems somehow unbelievable. They do not believe the baby will thrive unless there is something solid in its tummy.

Do babies thrive at the breast or not? Doctors are now questioning the practice of administering solids at an earlier and earlier age. The Committee on Nutrition showed how the trend went from no solids during the first year of life before the 1920s and then switched gradually into a cultural practice of introducing solids during the first days of life. In their report in 1958, the committee (representing the American Academy of Pediatrics) stated that

... lacking is proof obtained from controlled observations that feeding of solid food at ages earlier than 4 to 6 months of life is nutritionally or psychologically beneficial or, on the other hand, is actually harmful ... the feeding of solid foods nutritionally inferior to milk, at the expense of milk, could result in worsening the nutritional state of the infant rather than bettering it. . . . No harmful results have been reported thus far, but potential danger exists that earlier supplementation of the milk diets of infants with solid food of inferior nutritional content may, because of satiety, result in a decreased intake of milk.[5]

The early feeding of solids does not appear to have any rational basis. Dr. James Fruthaler from Ochsner Clinic, New Orleans, speaking at an annual medical meeting in 1964, said that a popular excuse for the giving of solids was to help the baby sleep through the night. He expressed concern over today's trend because the solids may actually increase the allergy potential in children.[6]

Other mothers say that they enjoy the longer interval between feedings. On the other hand, the baby does need frequent contact with his mother—at least more than every four hours.

Other reasons given for the early introduction of solids or supplementation are (1) the advertisements in lay and professional magazines, (2) the insistence of mothers or of doctors, and (3) the easy availability of baby cereals, pureed foods, and formulas.

Another factor that contributes to the early solids rush is our excessive concern for the baby's weight. More weight seems to be equated with better health. But is a fat baby necessarily a healthy baby? Back in 1958 Dr. Gilbert Forbes questioned the trend of overfeeding our infants, and he also questioned the early introduction of solids, for which there is no proven need.[7] In a recent issue

5. Committee on Nutrition, "On the Feeding of Solid Foods to Infants," *Pediatrics* 21 (1958): 686, 689, and 691.
6. James Fruthaler, "Solid Foods May Increase Allergy Potential in Infants," *Journal of the American Medical Association,* 190 (1964): 38.
7. Gilbert Forbes, "Do We Need a New Perspective in Infant Nutrition?," *Journal of Pediatrics,* 52 (1958): 496.

of a popular women's magazine Stanley Englebardt demonstrated through research and various medical opinions that overweight in an infant can lead to obesity in later life. Early overfeeding means the formation of more fat cells, cells a person keeps throughout his entire lifetime. Because of these additional fat cells, a fat baby will have greater difficulty staying slim in later years. He quoted several doctors who agreed that prevention of obesity begins in infancy, a time when eating habits are formed. One of the doctors he quoted, Dr. Virginia Vivian (a nutritionist from Ohio State University), stated that the first six months may be the most crucial in determining the number of fat cells.[8]

OTHER REASONS FOR WAITING

It is ironic that we have striven toward better nutrition and yet while doing so we have become indifferent to the merits of breast-feeding. Maybe the following material will offer you some encouragement and conviction in your desire to nurse your baby.

1. *Babies do gain well on breast milk alone.* Mothers often doubt this fact until they see it for themselves. One mother wrote, "I laugh now when I think of how I asked John if your babies were healthy and if they gained weight just nursing." Some mothers become concerned because their baby did not gain much by the first monthly visit, but even these mothers become confident as they observe with pride their growing breast-fed baby.

A 1964 study on weight gain was carefully conducted by several doctors and involved some 599 babies who were under observation for one year. A select group of 89 babies were completely nursed for six months (no vitamins and no solids were administered). Breast milk was their only intake. No signs of rickets or anemia were observed in this group of babies, even though no other source of vitamin D or iron was administered in the first six months of life and these babies were outside only during the warmer months of the year. The doctors found that this group of babies grew at the same rate as the other two groups of

8. Stanley Englebardt, "Are You Overfeeding Your Child?," *Woman's Day,* July 1971, p. 12.

babies under observation: (1) infants who were completely nursed for six months and received vitamin supplements and (2) infants who were bottle-fed and received vitamin supplements.[9]

2. *Breast-fed babies are healthier.* Dr. Robbins Kimball has observed that during the first ten years of life the breast-fed youngster is healthier and is more resistant to infections than a bottle-fed child. The bottle-fed child has "4 times the respiratory infections, 20 times the diarrhea, 22 times the miscellaneous infections, 8 times the eczema, 21 times the asthma, 27 times the hayfever" and he also had eleven times more tonsilectomies and four times more ear infections. In his study he also found the bottle-fed child had "11 times the hospital admissions and 8 times the house calls."[10]

Dr. Richard Applebaum in his book *Abreast of the Times* stresses the health benefits from colostrum by stating that this first milk (1) contains "natural antibodies against measles, polio, mumps and a host of other diseases"; (2) acts on a bacteria (*E. coli*) that "is notorious for causing infant diarrhea the first month of life" and may cause infantile meningitis; and (3) offers the baby "protection against respiratory infections, such as flu and pneumonia." During one cold winter he observed that of the babies who were brought into his office for colds, coughs, and high fevers none were breast-fed.[11]

While we lived in California our pediatrician was also impressed with the health of the breast-fed babies in his practice. This impression left him with the desire to learn more about breast-feeding, as he admitted having learned very little about it in medical school. He observed in his own work that the overall health of the breast-fed baby was superior to the overall health of the bottle-fed baby.

Jelliffe and Jelliffe conclude that "cow's milk preparations have no scientific advantage or superiority over human milk." The only advantage of a cow's milk preparation, as they see it, is its usefulness for the working mother; indeed, in some areas of the world

9. R. L. Jackson *et al.*, "Growth of 'Well-born' American Infants Fed Human and Cow's Milk," *Pediatrics* 33 (1964): 642.

10. Robbins E. Kimball, "How I Get Mothers to Breastfeed," *Physician's Management,* June 1968.

11. 1969, p. 11.

breast milk is a nutritional necessity for maintaining a healthy infant. From the research they conclude:

In less technically developed areas of the world, including under-privileged groups in industrialized countries, the antidiarrheal and nutritional importance of breast feeding is increasingly obvious, as the sole food for 4 to 6 months and as a small, but significant, protein supplement thereafter during the first 2 or more years of life. Ironically, at the same time, the disastrous trend to unaffordable artificial feeding continues in peri-urban areas, with increasing prevalence of marasmus and diarrhea in early infancy, a period of high vulnerability for immediate ill effects and long-term damage.[12]

The ill effects of artificial feeding have been observed in Jamaica, where mothers have switched to the bottle. Since the change from breast to bottle, many infants have become seriously sick with marasmus and kwashiokor.[13] The Jamaican government has already begun to initiate programs to educate and to encourage mothers to nurse their babies.[14]

At the Ninth International Congress of Nutrition the consensus among the doctors was that breast milk alone should be offered during the baby's first three to four months and that no supplements, solids, or other milks should be given during that time under any circumstances except emergencies. The doctors said that breast milk protects a child from obesity, diarrhea, staph, and other infections.[15]

Companies who manufacture baby foods are being severely criticized for adding unnecessary items to the jar's contents that may be harmful to the infant's health—namely, too much sugar, salt, and starch. The Consumer Union of the United States has informed the buying public that a high salt intake is associated with high blood pressure and other arterial diseases leading to heart problems. Sugar leads to dental decay. Not enough is known about the starches, but it is believed that obesity in the infant leads

12. D. B. Jelliffe and E. F. P. Jelliffe, "The Uniqueness of Human Milk," *The American Journal of Clinical Nutrition* 24 (August 1971): 1019.

13. Marasmus is a progressive wasting away, especially in infants, where there is no obvious cause. Kwashiokor is a protein-deficiency disease.

14. Betty Ann Countryman, Personal La Leche League newsletter of Jamaican trip in June 1970.

15. *The Cincinnati Enquirer*, September 9, 1972.

to overweight problems in the adult. In this most recent study the Consumer Union encourages mothers to make their own infant foods.[16] Of course, a mother who follows the natural inclinations of her child would not be bothered by buying or making special baby foods. Breast milk would suffice until the baby begins to help himself from the table.

Many of us have been acquainted with babies who require special formulas, which can be quite costly. This expense, of course, could have been avoided if the mother had been breast-feeding in the first place. There are also a few babies who would have died if breast milk had not been available to them. I would like to quote from two letters I received while in the process of writing this book.

Our league here has just had a rewarding experience in providing breastmilk for a very premature baby who could not tolerate formula and [his condition] was becoming very critical. The pediatrician called La Leche League as a last resort as the mother was not nursing. After being given breastmilk, the baby improved immediately and surpassed his birthweight of slightly over two pounds.

Right now we are supplying a baby with breast milk. He was three and a half months old and barely living at eight pounds in the University Hospital at Saskatoon when I was asked if we could provide breast milk for him. Now (a month later) he is a healthy eleven pounds fourteen ounces and growing at an unbelievable rate. The mother is trying to relactate but is having quite a bit of difficulty. . . . There is no doubt that this baby would have died had he not gotten breast milk.

3. *Breast-fed babies develop fewer allergies.* Dr. Frank Richardson, author of *The Nursing Mother,* said in 1953 that

delaying the addition of solid or semisolid foods until the baby is five or six months old does no harm; and giving them earlier probably serves no specially valuable purpose. . . . Furthermore, the allergists are almost unanimous in asserting that the earlier solid foods are introduced, the more likely a child is to become sensitized to them.[17]

Pediatrician Douglas Johnstone of the University of Rochester said in 1964 that early solids may be responsible for the current

16. "Baby Foods," *Consumer Reports,* October 1972.
17. Englewood Cliffs, N.J.: Prentice-Hall, 1953.

rise of allergies among children.[18] And Dr. Paul Gyorgy, a pediatrician who received the American Pediatric Society's annual Howland Award in 1968 for distinguished achievement, discouraged the early introduction of solids or supplements because these foods are the leading allergens among infants.[19]

At a gathering of physicians in 1972 Dr. John W. Gerrard, professor of pediatrics at the University of Saskatchewan, claimed that 7 percent of all babies are allergic to cow's milk in various degrees. It may manifest itself by a mild wheezing, an eczema, or persistent colds. Some children fortunately outgrow their allergy, and can eventually drink milk products.[20]

Breast-fed babies also have less diaper rash. Mothers who have bottle-fed previous babies and then switched to breast-feeding for a later baby have found that the breast-fed baby requires less care. These mothers have found that they can use plastic pants, change diapers at longer intervals, and only occasionally dip into the Vaseline jar. By comparison, with previous babies they went through jar after jar of Vaseline and had to change diapers more frequently.

4. *Breast-feeding saves time.* Time that isn't spent in the kitchen preparing bottles, nipples, and formula or spent in cleaning up afterwards is time saved. Breast-feeding means food for the baby that takes no time to prepare and only a little time to serve. It's even quicker than an "instant breakfast," but who's in a rush anyway? The food is ready any time or anywhere for the asking and is always at the right temperature. There is no need to warm it up or cool it down. Instead of work, it means "little" breaks during the day to sit down (or lie down) and enjoy the children God gave you.

Breast-feeding generally means fewer visits to the doctor or hospital. It means less work for a sick mother who can care for her baby in bed. It may mean less work for the physically handicapped mother who would also enjoy this intimate contact with her baby. It means one hand free to hug a child, answer the phone, or eat a meal.

18. Douglas Johnstone, "Early Solid Feeding Called Allergy Factor," *Medical World News*, 1964.

19. Paul Gyorgy, "Trends and Advances in Infant Nutrition," *The West Virginia Medical Journal*, April 1957.

20. *St. Paul Dispatch,* March 7, 1972.

Breast-feeding means carefree traveling with no special baby stops, whether it's a day outing for the family, a week's vacation or a trip to Europe. For campers, it's the best way to travel with a baby.

5. *Breast-feeding saves money.* Money not spent on bottles, nipples, brushes, sterilizer, formula, juice, foods, food and bottle warmers, and the gas or electricity required in the preparation is money saved. In the years to come it usually means less money spent on doctor's fees, hospital fees, and probably fewer drugs and fewer dental bills. Breast-feeding costs nothing except tender loving care.

Nursing mothers have figured out that, when a mother nurses her baby completely for the entire first six months, the savings add up to $150 to $200. Our estimate was generous toward the bottle-feeding mother, for we assumed that she would not begin solids until her baby was three months old and that she would not be using an expensive brand of bottle or formula.

6. *Nature has a diet plan for your baby.* The presence of a strong sucking reflex and the absence of teeth are physical signs indicating that nature intended babies to have milk in the first months of life. Later, some physical changes occur. The teeth begin to come in at a very slow pace, and the swallowing reflex has developed. Baby has already started manipulating anything he can grasp toward his mouth. All of these changes suggest that baby will soon be ready to grab food off the table. The Committee on Nutrition has said that

the rooting and sucking reflex exhibited in the newborn, and persisting for many months, would indicate that this is the normal method by which the infant obtains food. . . . Salivary secretion, as manifested by

110

drooling, usually does not make its appearance until the third or fourth month. Teeth appear around 6 months of age and chewing motions are a later accomplishment. All of these are indicative of nature's plan for a liquid diet for the first few months of life.[21]

The timing involved with the eruption of the first set of teeth may correspond closely to the time of partial breast-feeding. Normally, babies are physiologically ready for solids at about the time when their first teeth are making an appearance. Likewise, the baby gradually weans himself off the breast during the months that he is gradually completing his first set of teeth. Both the weaning period and the eruption period are normally completed toward the end of the baby's second year, when the feeding of an infant follows a natural course. The above relationship, however, is a general one. Some babies will have teeth at three months but will not be ready for solids until six months; others will be ready for solids at six months and not have teeth until twelve months of age. This general observation might explain why they used to call the first set of teeth "milk" teeth.

One study showed that babies who accepted solids willingly at an early age might refuse them later. The general reaction of babies to early solids was studied by Virginia Beal of the Child Research Council. She said that "the most common picture is one of eagerness for the bottle but resistance to feeding of other foods, with crying or fussing or spitting out, until a time, usually between 4 or 6 months of age, when the child begins to accept willingly the solid fools."[22]

Even when babies are good eaters at one or two months of age, mothers still say that it's a lot of unnecessary bother. And besides, it usually means giving him less and less of the best food, which you alone can offer him.

7. *Baby and mother thrive on each other.* The emotional benefits of breast-feeding are valued as highly as the physical benefits by many doctors and experts today. More and more emphasis is being placed on the importance of skin-to-skin contact between

21. *Op. cit.*, p. 690.
22. Virginia Beal, "On the Acceptance of Solid Foods, and Other Food Patterns, of Infants and Children," *Pediatrics* 20 (1957): 448.

parent and child—whether it be in the act of nursing a baby, rubbing a child's back, or rocking a child to sleep. Physical contact generates warm feelings of being loved and appreciated. With breast-feeding the child is guaranteed frequent contact with his mother. Dr. Grantly Dick-Read has written:

What are three things these children require and thrive on? (1) They are born to seek food at once from the mother's breast . . . (2) They desire warmth from the mother's body. And then, perhaps what is more important: (3) They need security in their mother's presence. These three factors are the only provision that nature demands all children should have for their first weeks of neonatal life. Breastfeeding satisfies all three.[23]

The emotional benefits flowing from the breast-feeding act are just as important to the mother. The National Research Council asked "whether the contact with the infant which breastfeeding provides is not equally as desirable, and even necessary, for the mother as for the infant. It gives a mother a feeling of satisfaction, security, and trust in herself which she needs in the future care of her child."[24]

Breast-feeding is a very satisfying and enjoyable experience for the nursing mother. It grows on her, and she seems to enjoy it more as the baby grows older and as she has other babies. This is probably the main reason why many mothers are so enthusiastic about nursing. Articles and letters have been written by bottle-feeding parents in reaction against these breast-feeding enthusiasts. They defend their choice to bottle-feed because they love their children and are trying to be good parents. This is true; they are good and loving parents, but there still is a difference. I have never yet heard of a mother who cried when her baby was weaned from the bottle. But from the breast, yes!

23. Grantly Dick-Read, *Childbirth Without Fear,* 4th Edition (New York: Harper & Row, 1972), p. 92.
24. National Research Council, *Maternal Nutrition,* p. 163.

10

Nursing the Older Child

NATURE'S NORM

Experience has shown that the mother who follows this book's pattern of natural mothering will usually be nursing well beyond her baby's first birthday. In our survey of breast-feeding and amenorrhea, the group that followed this pattern averaged 14.6 months of amenorrhea but continued nursing and averaged almost 23.0 months of breast-feeding. This meant, then, that over 40 percent nursed beyond the child's second birthday and a few went close to and beyond the third birthday. The cover article of *La Leche League News* for November–December 1972 was about a "happy, healthy, talkative four-year-old" boy who had nursed until about three months short of his fourth birthday. Thus it is evident that some normal American women are experiencing the same kind of extended natural mothering pattern that is common in cultures that are very much in touch with nature. In this chapter we will use the term "older child" to refer to the baby who has passed his first birthday, and we'll be looking at some reasons for nursing the older child, some cultural attitudes, and some ways for the long-term nursing mother to find support when some of the other gals tell her she's a nut.

In our culture it is expected that a baby will be weaned from the breast at least by ten months of age or by the time he begins to walk. The nine- or ten-month period following childbirth is a common time for nursing mothers to wean. In our survey, out of the entire group, 25.0 percent weaned between nine and twelve months (the most common time in our survey) and 20.6 percent weaned between thirteen and sixteen months (the next most common time). This, keep in mind, was from a group of women interested enough in breast-feeding to have read the first, privately published edition of this book.

It must be remembered that people are not used to hearing of women who nurse longer than a year, and that, secondly, most people have a very limited view of breast-feeding. There are those who look at breast-feeding only in terms of nutrition or those who see it only as a means of birth control. If you look at breast-feeding as a way of satisfying baby's hunger pains, then you can readily see why a baby could be weaned by ten months. With the introduction of solids and early use of the cup, breast-feeding is no longer necessary except for medical reasons (e.g., allergies). And, for those who look upon breast-feeding primarily as a means of avoiding a pregnancy, once menstruation resumes there is no reason to continue the nursing relationship. However, even some of those who are most adamant about breast-feeding in the early months for the full range of nutritional and emotional reasons are either shocked or surprised to learn that a mother is nursing an older child. On the other hand, if breast-feeding involves a whole method of child care and if the breast is looked upon as a wonderful mothering tool, then there is no need to have a cut-off date. A mother may as well take advantage of this easy form of mothering while she can. Two or three years of nursing may sound like a long time, but in terms of the child's lifetime it is brief.

Unfortunately, some people will find cruel explanations for prolonged nursing. They may say that the mother is smothering the child or that she is nursing for sexual kicks. Some will infer that she is using the baby as a birth-control device. They will worry that the mother is being neglectful or that the baby will be psychologically damaged. Will the baby boy grow up to be feminine or will the child have homosexual tendencies? Is the baby addicted to the breast? The above fears appear to be unfounded. In fact, the widely publicized incidence of homosexuality occurs in an age of bottle-feeding and early weaning practices.

Certainly, prolonged breast-feeding is not accountable in our society for this incidence. In the light of the severely critical comments that are sometimes made, it is helpful to have the support of others when you are nursing the child according to his own timetable for nursing.

NURSING NEEDS OF THE OLDER CHILD

Maria Montessori supports nature's guidelines for mothering. Her views about early infant care are well expressed in her book *The Absorbent Mind*. She advises parents to respect the child's natural development. "Localized states of maturity must first be established, and the effort to force the child's natural development can only do harm. It is nature that directs. Everything depends on her and must obey her command."[1]

Once a mother has decided to go along with her baby and let him wean himself, at his own pace, she may have some second thoughts. Perhaps she thought this meant a couple of extra months —and now he's almost two. Could he possibly still have a need for breast-feeding? Interestingly enough, we see nothing strange in a two-year-old using a bottle or a pacifier. Because the long-term nursing mother is an exception in our culture, the doubts persist. She can take comfort in these passages from Eda LeShan's *How Do Your Children Grow?*

We also have to understand, and this holds true all through parenthood, that when a need is met, it goes away. Children of any age do not continue to behave in certain ways unless there is a need. When they are finished with it, they will give it up. Sometimes it may go on longer than we expect, and a parent will worry because a three-year-old is not completely toilet trained, or will be concerned because a sixteen-month-old is still nursing. This is a very natural tendency. We think the things that are happening will go on forever. The truth is that they will go on only as they are needed.[2]

However, we worry far too much about the need lasting too long. That is less likely to do any damage than the opposite, cutting it off too quickly. The one thing that upsets parents and children more than any-

1. New York: Dell, 1967, p. 88.
2. New York: David McKay, 1972, pp. 17–18.

thing else is the unfinished business of any one phase of life. If a child needs to go through some kind of an emotional experience, and he doesn't go through it at the time that is most appropriate, it is never finished.[3]

Prolonged breast-feeding may also prove helpful in emergency situations or during an illness. Temporary emergency situations, such as car trouble or bad weather conditions, may cause a period of isolation during which nursing would be advantageous. Prolonged breast-feeding may influence your baby's health even after his first birthday. The older baby who loses his appetite during an illness will at least receive good nourishment from the breast at a time when he might not take any other foods. Here is a story of one mother who was grateful that she had continued to nurse her child:

When our second son was being seen by his pediatrician for his first yearly checkup, the doctor questioned me about his still being nursed. "Aren't you ever going to wean him? You know, he's not needing this physically for nutrition anymore." I answered, "Great! I'll go home with a pacified doctor and a very frustrated baby." We both laughed and I assured the doctor that he would wean—but at *his* own rate.

Two months later, the baby became ill with an intestinal virus. His fever was 105 and we rushed him to the hospital. For two days and nights he was kept on clear liquids and nursing. Even with this, the diarrhea was so severe that the doctor ordered IV's to prevent further dehydration. This lasted forty-eight hours. During this period I couldn't even nurse him. Actually, he was so sick that he slept most of the time —so I was the one who suffered, with full breasts.

Hand expressing and pumping with the breast pump somehow just didn't seem to empty my breasts as completely as a baby nursing does. I'm certain that a good deal of it was psychological for me, too. By the end of the second day the doctor asked me, "Do you think he still remembers how to nurse after this long? If he does and *since* it's breast milk—I'll let him have the milk. I know he'll regain his strength faster. Also it won't upset his intestines like 'foreign' milk would." Still remember how? You don't practice something several times a day for fourteen months and then forget in two days! I only wish I had words to describe how eagerly he settled against me—knowing *exactly* where he was going. Joy and relief flooded us both!

3. *Ibid.*, p. 18.

Later during a visit to the doctor's office, the pediatrician gave me one of the nicest compliments I ever had with a nursing experience: "You've shown me how important it is to follow a baby-led weaning pattern, and never will I pressure a mother about weaning again."

The most common reason given for prolonged breast-feeding is the special relationship that a mother has with her child. This closeness is strengthened over a period of two or three years through the nursing relationship, and it cannot easily be lost once the breast-feeding comes to an end. The bond is still there, and a mother can maintain it through other avenues of affection and communication, physical or verbal. One wonders whether the "generation gap" begins at such an early time. Would more parents be in tune with their children if they had breast-fed for a considerable length of time? Would children be more sensitive to their parents' feelings if they had experienced this long-term relationship with the one parent in early childhood?

Certainly there are other factors that can influence our relationships with our children, but today we parents need all the help we can get to do a better job of raising our children. We also need easier methods, and breast-feeding, at least, makes the job easier during those early years. Whether it helps in later years is speculative. At this writing our children are still young, but I often find myself grateful to breast-feeding for the relationships that exist in our family. The children have a caring concern for their parents and for each other. Other parents, too, have told us that there is a bond and closeness with their breast-fed child that they didn't achieve when they bottle-fed. This closeness has also matured them, and given them a deeper appreciation of the needs of their older children and even of other children in the immediate neighborhood.

The warm relationship that develops during the first years as part of the natural mothering program certainly is a big help in developing open communications. I am not suggesting that the mother who lets her children breast-feed into the second, third, or fourth year will have no communication problems with them in the teen years. What I am suggesting, however, is that the close relationship and the habit of being open to the young child's needs provide an excellent start. The parents who maintain this habit of openness to the child's needs should have less difficulty during those adolescent years. One mother wrote:

My second oldest child was fifteen yesterday, and as I look back as I have done repeatedly in the last ten years since my joy of discovering breast-feeding, I'm still regretful about those years of bottle-feeding with my first three children. It is said that you don't cry over spilt milk, but I do, and I think that is my underlying motivation in trying to help other mothers and families.

We have all heard various psychologists say something to the effect that a child's character or the way he will respond to different situations is pretty much set by the time he enters kindergarten. If during a good half of those years he found security and warmth at his mother's breast, as he needed it and not as someone else dictated, then this would seem to be a good foundation of trust for the later years. To put it another way, if the parents have really been giving of themselves in the early years and have not forced later childhood and its greater independence on a baby or young child whose own pace is not yet ready for full weaning, then perhaps the favor may be returned in later years; perhaps when that child reaches adolescence, he will not force himself into that radical independence that is the bane of many a teen-ager's parents' existence; perhaps in return for his parents' earlier acceptance of his own pace, he will now accept a gradual pace himself and will not strive for full independence before he is ready for it.

Certainly these last thoughts are more speculative than factually based. However, hopeful and ignorant of the future as we are, the fact still remains that as parents of young children we are called to respond to their needs with ourselves, and not just with things that money can buy. Doing our best for the child, giving him the best of everything, doesn't mean only clothes, schools, toys, transportation, vacations, lessons, tutors, baby-sitters, and money. As Dr. James L. Hymes, Jr., tells us in *The Child Under Six*, "One way or another adults must help themselves to realize what is our adult job—to give to children. Not things, but ourselves. We give our time, our love, our care. Babies cannot do for themselves. We have to be on hand, gladly, to meet their needs."[4]

4. Englewood Cliffs, N.J.: Prentice-Hall, 1961, p. 61.

There is no doubt that while natural mothering at times is more convenient than using artifacts, it also takes time; best of all, it always gives individual attention, which may be looked upon as a wise investment in the child's future.

Margaret Mead, in an excellent article, "Working Mothers and Their Children," expressed concern over the type of care the young child receives in day care centers: "Only individual attention can turn a child into a full human being, capable of growth." She criticized a frequent change in the mother-figure and noted that a small child "needs someone who is intensely interested in him or her, who will spend endless hours responding and initiating, repeating sounds, noting nuances of expression, reinforcing new skills, bolstering self-confidence and a sense of self." A child who receives such continuity, she claims, "can survive a great many changes of place and person later." Persons who have not had such care "have less capacity to trust the world, to leave home happily, and to form wider and more intense relationships with other people later."[5] Considering the many changes of place and persons that some children experience in our mobile society, the individual time and attention spent in natural mothering is a sound investment.

I think there are other benefits of prolonged nursing that lets the child wean at his own pace. Natural breast-feeding helps the parent to accept the child for what he is. Instead of imposing outside norms, natural mothering looks to the inner growth pattern of the child. The child's growth in all its phases is specially guarded and respected. These phases of growth are not forced to end too early, nor are they forced to remain when the need is no longer

5. *Catholic World*, November 1970, p. 78.

present. This acceptance and love for the child as he is may help the parents to accept him at his own level of interests and development in later years.

Another tremendous benefit from prolonged breast-feeding is the stimulation that the child receives when his mother takes him with her. He is exposed to a wide variety of social circumstances and, in addition, he has the security of his parents or his mother wherever he goes. This stimulation is probably far greater than that which he would receive by remaining at home with sitters.

By no means least among the benefits of prolonged nursing is the continuation of family-centeredness. In the family where ecological breast-feeding is used in the first year, the baby is always a part of the family; the parents don't take off and leave him. Likewise when the mother continues to let her baby nurse beyond the first year, she will not be leaving him for extended periods of time. Instead, she will want to be near him, and she and her husband will plan recreation activities that are family oriented. The child who grows up in such a family today is lucky indeed. Family life in America is such that professionals are becoming concerned: it is too common for parents to look upon children as a burden or as second-class citizens within the family; the parents are constantly striving to get away from their children. The extended nursing of natural mothering is a tendency in the other direction.

SOME CHARACTERISTICS OF THE OLDER NURSING CHILD

What can you expect from the older nursing child? First, you will find that your child will ask for the breast at any time or place. In fact, he may ask for it at a time when you do not want him to ask, when you are around strangers or new relatives and friends. This presents a new environment to the child, and, in looking for security from his mother, he often seeks it at the breast.

You can avoid some embarrassment for yourself by having the child call the breast "ma-ma" or "mum-mum" or any word other than that which resembles a word like "nursie." You may also not call it anything; your child will simply inform you of his intentions by pulling or tugging at your top. If other persons are around, they will probably not pick up the clue. You can leave temporarily to nurse or explain the situation to the company or hostess. If you are away from home, the hostess can lead you into a more secluded area, such as her bedroom or den.

Of course, under some circumstances you could nurse on the spot without offending people or feeling funny but such situations are rare today. You will find that it is harder to nurse modestly with a bigger baby. He is too big for blankets; thus, the blanket can't be used as a shield. There is also a good chance he will dislike clothing too close to his face. He may pull at your bra or clothing in a playful manner, so that attention is actually drawn toward the nursing area. An older child may touch or lay his hand on the other breast while nursing, and this may offend people. Considering the situation, it is usually best to nurse only among those who understand and appreciate this type of mothering.

You will note other changes as you nurse the older child. He is talkative, playful, and affectionate. His responses are greatly varied. At times he will even tell you where to nurse him! There is also more give and take. He can appreciate the fact that you are busy and can wait a few minutes for a nursing. He may also be able to learn to wait that one hour during church service.

You can also expect nursing sprees. Some days you will wonder why your child wants to nurse every hour for a few minutes or why the child wants to nurse almost continuously during the night. We noticed, for example, that after we moved to another state our three-year-old nursed almost constantly during the night for several weeks. Sometimes it can be explained and other times it can't be explained, but trust that this will pass in due time and the child will reduce the frequency. In fact, in due time trust that your child will no longer want you in this way. The relationship, however, is enjoyable and you will not be anxious to see it come to an end. Under nature's program the transition through months and months of gradual weaning is so slow that you are ready to end the nursing relationship when the time comes.

As your child reaches the age of two and a half or three years, you will soon find that he will not want to nurse in front of others who are strange to him. He will prefer to nurse only in front of family members. He may not want his parents or brothers and sisters to discuss his nursing with others in his presence or to tattle to his friends. His wishes should be respected within the family.

You may also find that your child is still nursing frequently in spite of being older. In writing and talking with other mothers, I find that it is common for older children reaching their second or even third birthday to be nursing quite frequently still. Some people feel that if a child has other brothers or sisters to keep him busy, or if a mother keeps her child interested in other activities, the child will lose interest in the breast. I find little support for this view. In the busiest of households and with mothers who stimulate their youngsters toward various activities, the child will still take the time to nurse in the midst of it all.

Night feedings can be expected while your older child is still nursing. In our study of mothers who nursed in a manner similar to the natural mothering program, most mothers nursed for as many months as they gave night feedings. They averaged almost twenty-four months of night feedings; the real average would be an even longer time, since a little over 50 percent were still giving night feedings at the time of the survey. Usually the last feedings to be dropped are those related to sleep. Therefore, toward the end of his nursing career the child will be nursing before naptime or before bedtime in the evening. His last feeding may occur in the middle of the night. If this situation does happen, then no one except your husband will know that your child is still nursing—unless you tell them.

FINAL WEANING

In natural mothering the time of final weaning is unpredictable, because it is at the child's own pace. Sometimes a mother expects to nurse a baby for about two years only to be surprised to find her child weaned much earlier. Such a mother must realize that mothering isn't limited to the breast but that there are other ways to meet his needs. She can still provide body contact and lots of love and do many things with him. She can be assured that she satisfied his needs at the breast. On the other hand, there are other children who will be on only a few nursings a day for a long period of time before they gradually lose interest. A few mothers may feel guilty that their child doesn't nurse as frequently as Mrs. Jones's baby, and they will be disappointed when their baby refuses the breast. I think the main point to remember is to enjoy your baby and *his* schedule. Contented mothering is the goal, not competitive mothering.

THE EXAMPLE OF OTHERS

Despite the many benefits that mothers have found to be associated with the extended nursing of natural mothering, it is still a difficult thing even to consider in our culture. Most people will not appreciate long-term nursing unless they have done it, have known a close friend or relative who has done it, or have found themselves in the situation where it was evident that their baby still desired to be at the breast. The desire to nurse an older baby often comes by way of example. A mother can be encouraged to continue nursing her child if she knows of another mother who is nursing an older baby. Other mothers have wanted to nurse longer but quit because they knew of no one else who was doing it.

Your own feelings about nursing the older child will change as your nursing experience develops or matures with age. Reasons for prolonged lactation will probably play a small part in this change of attitudes. What will change your feelings on the subject at the time will be that one-year-old or two-year-old in your arms who still needs you. The pressures from society to wean may encourage you to stall a feeding only to find tears rolling down your child's cheeks—and you lovingly take him to breast. Secondly, the relationship is too enjoyable for its ending to be hastened, so you will find yourself learning to appreciate a new dimension in it.

THE WORKING MOTHER

Some mothers who are involved in continued nursing may find themselves in a situation where it is necessary to go back to work. I know of mothers who have remained at home when their children were young in spite of financial difficulties; yet it can't be ignored that for some families financial difficulties will occur and the mother may find it necessary to provide some source of income for her family. One possibility is working within the home by taking care of other children, by doing telephone surveys, and so forth. Another possibility is finding part-time work where the mother is gone only a few days or for only four hours during the day. We chose to do this once when an unforeseen difficulty developed. Our youngest was still nursing at two years of age, and I worked for a brief period of time at a place within walking distance of our home and for only two afternoons a week. My husband was also able to arrange to be home those working afternoons.

Some mothers cannot arrange part-time work; their only choice is full-time employment. Full-time employment does not mean you have to wean your baby or older child. Try to arrange a situation where you can be with your child during the lunch hour, either by working near home or where your child will be taken care of during your working hours. The reason it is nice to be close to your child in distance is that he can be nursed during the lunch break. For a small baby the nursing at lunchtime could be very important; in addition, it helps to be relieved of your milk. One mother wrote me saying that her older baby soon learned that she would be coming at lunchtime and after work, and he quickly started refusing the bottle; instead he would wait for her. Another working mother enjoyed sleeping with her nursing baby, since she was well rested for work the following day. The most important considerations to make when employment looks imminent are how to continue having this special relationship with your child and how to offer him the best possible care and security while you are away.

HOSPITALIZATION

Other mothers are confronted with hospitalization, either for herself or for the child. Again, there is usually no need to consider weaning. One close friend arranged to be with her totally breast-fed baby during his hospital stay by leaving her two children with a grandmother who lived fairly close to the hospital. She could not stay with him during the night but she was allowed to remain with him during the day and until he went to sleep at night. She also managed to make quick trips to eat meals with her children. Another friend did not leave her nursing two-year-old at all during his hospital stay.

A nursing mother was hospitalized recently for two and a half days as a result of surgery. Arrangements were made with the hospital so that her husband could bring her two-year-old to her six times during her stay. This mother also found it helpful to distribute La Leche League's reprints on weaning[6] to interested nurses and hospital personnel. Another nursing mother was allowed to have her own mother present following surgery to carry the baby to her for feedings. The baby was then allowed to remain with the mother.

Whether a mother is bottle-feeding or breast-feeding, hospitalization of mother or baby will be hard on both, especially when the relationship is a close one. More parents are requesting that they be allowed to stay with their child, and more hospitals are providing rooming-in arrangements for one parent. Usually the hospital will make allowances when there is a special request. It would also be wise for the mother who cannot remain overnight to explain to the nurses that her child has not had a bottle and suggest offering expressed breast milk by spoon or by cup. If the nurse is informed about your baby, she will be more understanding of the situation and will not get upset if the baby refuses the bottle. Psychological studies, however, do show that a child is better off during his hospital stay when his mother can remain with him.[7]

LONG-TERM NURSING IN THE AMERICAN CULTURE

How can you handle the reaction of others with respect to long-range nursing? First of all, you can appreciate why others feel the way they do about prolonged nursing when you try to picture yourself nursing someone else's older child. I have nursed an older child—my own—yet I dislike the idea of nursing some-

6. Edwina Froehlich, "Thoughts About Weaning," La Leche League reprint, from *Newsletter* 1, no. 5.
7. John Bowlby, *Child Care and the Growth Of Love* (Baltimore: Penguin Books, 1953), pp. 175–180.

one else's child who is one or two years old. I can easily picture myself, however, nursing other small babies. What makes the difference in one's feeling with regard to the older age is the fact that this is your child. There is a special relationship that you would want to have with only your child.

Then you should realize that the relative infrequency of long-term nursing is in itself a cause of unfavorable reactions. Some people are unfavorably impressed by almost anything out of the ordinary. And a great number of otherwise well-educated people are simply amazed to learn that a mother can still be producing milk two and three years after childbirth.

Because your audience will most likely think you're crazy, there's no reason in the world why you have to volunteer information. Don't tell them that you are still nursing if you don't have to. If a situation develops where you find you have to tell, my husband and I have found that the best policy in handling other persons' questions is usually to be honest and "sure-headed." You will discover that there is very little static or none at all when you convey the attitude that you are confident in what you are doing and that you feel that this is the way it should be done. If you don't like to give personal reasons, you can always refer to women in other parts of the world and to those American women who nursed for several years before the "bottle" generations. Other mothers have found it extremely helpful to throw the attention to another nursing mother by saying, "I have a friend who is nursing a child who is even older than ours." If you do know of someone who is nursing a child older than yours, you will find that this offers you a great deal of support. The best support a nursing mother can have, however, is her husband. If her husband is 100 percent behind her, then an unkind remark will not hurt nearly as badly. It is wonderful to have a husband step in and handle the discussion, especially when the reactions are quite strong.

In the last analysis, if you are engaged in prolonged nursing because your child still wants to nurse and not out of some personal whim "to show the world" or to compete with somebody else, if you recognize that this is common in many cultures of the world, and if your husband supports you, then you have nothing to fear. On the other hand, you should not look down on the mother who is engaged in the child care typical of American culture. Ignorance is usually the greatest barrier to freedom. A person can't choose something before she knows about it, and most American women have never been exposed to the ideas we call natural mothering.

Today we have much talk about changing life styles, some of which concerns a return to nature. This doesn't mean that we have to move out of the city, or that everybody has to have an organic garden. Nature isn't to be found just in the fields and the forest or among the animals. Though our nature is incomparably higher and more complex than that of the animal and vegetable kingdoms, we still have a nature and we are better off when we live according to it instead of going against it.

Obviously there are different degrees of living with or going against our common human nature. I think that almost everyone would agree with me that the parents who killed their child would be going against our human nature in a most serious way; the same would be said about those who abused their child by beating or by seriously neglecting him. I would like to suggest that there are more subtle ways of going against our human nature, or at least of not really living in accord with it, and that this is particularly true in a culture that is fascinated by technology and "being modern." That fascination brought in the bottle and all but eliminated breast-feeding in America. Fortunately, there are an increasing number of people who recognize the wisdom of fostering the natural, at least when it comes to the early months of breast-feeding.

What we need is a life style that incorporates a new respect for living in full accord with our human nature. For the present, this will also demand a new independence from the dictates of our contemporary culture. Such a life style would support the close ties between a mother and her nursing child for as long as the child's needs kept him nursing. Since our present culture is not supportive of such a life style, it is all the more important for every nursing mother to have loving support from her husband. When he is really with you, it matters little what others may think.

On the other hand, if a husband is indifferent or even hostile to the idea of breast-feeding and prolonged nursing, then other support may be in vain. Therefore it is extremely important that a nursing mother be a communicating wife to her husband. She should share not only her conclusions but likewise her reasons and the materials that she has found helpful and convincing. Many husbands will have open (or at least secret) admiration for a wife's ability to make an intelligent case for extended nursing. Others will give their support if they see that the wife herself is really convinced and wants her husband's support regardless of how good a case she makes. What is important is that this be a shared decision so that the husband will be proud of his wife's willingness and desire to take care of their baby's needs in this way and so that the wife will find the support necessary to persevere in the face of cultural customs.

The strongest case for natural mothering and prolonged nursing is made by mothers who have raised one baby by our cultural standards and a later one according to the pattern of natural mothering. Repeatedly, those who changed their attitudes and allowed prolonged breast-feeding have found it to be a rewarding experience. It has been common for them to state that they wished they had nursed their previous children in a similar manner and that they feel that mothers are missing out on a valuable experience by weaning too early.

Thus far I have said almost nothing about prolonged breast-feeding and natural child spacing. However, I have mentioned previously that the women in our survey who followed close to the guidelines of natural mothering experienced an average of 14.6 months of amenorrhea; a few went up to and beyond two years. There is no way of predicting the length of amenorrhea for any particular woman whether in the first year or the second year. The late return of fertility and menstruation will usually happen only in those women who let their babies continue to nurse and who have the body chemistry factors that are favorable to a later return.

11

Personal Experiences

There is ample research to show that the breast-feeding program described in these pages will normally be effective in child spacing, but most people are not going to review the sources I have quoted. Most of us learn best by example. Thus I have included the following experiences from friends who initially took an interest in the subject of natural child spacing and who helped me develop my ideas about natural mothering. Although these experiences occurred at a time when the primary emphasis was on child spacing through the total nutrition rule, their stories show that they were grateful for both the natural infertility and the nursing experience in itself.

Their experiences likewise led me to write this book. For some reason, the physicians attending these women either did not or could not supply them with the information they needed at the time. They were most grateful for the information they received during our many conversations; and since this information was not available in book form, they encouraged me to put what we talked about into print.

MOTHER A

Mrs. A completely nursed her baby for five months before gradually introducing solids to her baby. Her first menstrual period occurred when her baby, her fifth child, was fourteen and one-half months of age.

At about three months following delivery Mrs. A spotted, and the same thing occurred twenty-eight days later. Her obstetrician did not believe in the spacing benefit of breast-feeding and told her that her periods were trying to return. She and I were both puzzled by the spotting, as her baby was completely breast-fed. Finally I asked her when she fed the baby during the night. She replied that her baby went to sleep early in the evening and awoke in the morning, quite content to go without an immediate feeding. We both felt that this long lapse in time may have been the cause of the spotting. She then took my suggestion to nurse her baby before retiring or else first thing in the morning. There were nights when her baby was too sleepy to nurse, and then there were nights when he demanded a night feeding. She also tried to increase his daytime feedings. No further signs of spotting or bleeding occurred until ten months later, when she had her first regular period. Menstruation, in this case, was absent during the latter nine months when the mother was weaning her baby. Her baby weaned himself at seventeen months of age.

Mrs. A could not convince her personal physician of the merit of breast-feeding in the area of family planning. As for her pediatrician, she was very reluctant to tell him that she was still nursing her baby. At the sixth-month checkup, she expressed her feelings on the matter, and expected that he would advise her to stop nursing. But to her surprise the doctor sat down, asked her some questions, and then admitted that he wished all the mothers of his little patients would do exactly as she was doing.

Mr. and Mrs. A's previous babies had been born about a year apart. They were happy to have learned about natural spacing, for they do want a larger family at a somewhat slower rate, and both like the natural way of doing things.

MOTHER B

Mrs. B nursed her baby completely for five months. Soon, after some solids were introduced, spotting occurred. The mother returned to complete breast-feeding and about two months later reintroduced solids because her baby wanted them. A regular period soon followed when her baby was eight months old. This was her fifth baby.

Mrs. B did not believe that breast-feeding would postpone another pregnancy. However, after reading the research and realizing that it is the sucking that is so important, she became convinced—and also was upset that her doctor hadn't told her about natural spacing with her first baby.

Mrs. B had several comments as regards the early return of menstruation after she introduced solids to her baby. First, she felt that the pacifier was her drawback. Since her baby used the pacifier regularly, he was never content to remain at the breast; her baby would not fall into a deep sleep at the breast like other babies. Maybe this additional pacifying-type sucking would have been all that was needed or required in order to hold back menstruation for a longer period of time after the baby began solids.

Secondly, she often used these solids to pacify the baby when all the baby wanted was her. If she was too busy to hold the baby, she found it more convenient to offer food to satisfy him. She came to regard this as a poor form of mothering. It also tended to limit the amount of sucking at the breast by filling up the baby with solids.

Mrs. B found several advantages in complete breast-feeding:

1. She was extremely happy to have learned about natural spacing and to have had peace of mind during the nonmenstrual phase of breast-feeding.

2. With her other babies she had found carrying them during menstruation very uncomfortable because of pain in her legs. However, with her last baby this did not occur. Also, by the time most nursing mothers' periods resume, their babies are learning how to walk and do not need to be carried as much around the house. She feels that other mothers who are uncomfortable during menses would also benefit by nursing properly and experiencing a lengthy absence from menstruation.

3. Mrs. B strongly feels that the children are the ones who benefit immensely from the extra contact and attention that is part of natural mothering. She feels it is so much easier to do this when they are little than to try to make up for it in later years. Frequently when babies are born close together, the parents tend to treat the older baby as a grown child and fail to realize that they really have two babies in the house—both of whom need lots of babying and loving care.

4. And, lastly, she feels that, if she had totally breast-fed in the early months, she would have been able to nurse her other babies. Early introduction of bottles and solids was the cause of her nursing failures. At this writing her baby looks as if he will be an early weaner; at ten months of age her baby only nurses well once during the day. The baby quickly lost interest in the breast once solids were introduced. Mrs. B plans to nurse until the baby weans himself; she is enjoying the relationship too much to stop and she feels that babies should be nursed for about two years. Since in her locality it is extremely rare to hear of a mother still nursing a baby at even ten months of age, she doesn't plan to advertise the fact. "I don't feel I have to explain myself to others or want to be in a position where I have to think up some reasons. I just want to and it's as simple as that."

MOTHER C

Mrs. C, a pharmacist from Australia, nursed her baby, her second child, "completely" for seven months. Her periods returned when her baby was nine months old.

Since she wanted to quit nursing at three months for fear of becoming pregnant—a common belief that has unfortunately developed out of the cultural breast-feeding practices that normally do not provide a lengthy period of natural infertility—Mrs. C began to offer her baby formula. The pediatrician asked her why she wanted to stop nursing, since her baby was allergic to other milks, and he then told her about proper breast-feeding in order to delay another pregnancy. He also told her that it would probably mean delaying solids for some time and then referred her to me.

As a pharmacist, this mother became extremely interested in the research material on the subject. She then remembered that her grandmother nursed all her children for two to three years and said it was the *only* way, and that her mother's advice was, "Be careful when you wean." She soon learned that in her home town in her native country a new instruction program on family planning had begun. The doctors spoke to parents at a public gathering, and free counseling appointments could be arranged privately with a doctor for those who desired them. What interested this mother was the fact that a letter from home mentioned that total breast-feeding was recommended in the doctors' presentation.

It is interesting to note that Mrs. C's baby went an unusual length of time between feedings for a breast-fed baby. Her baby nursed every four to six hours during the day, whereas most babies may nurse several times during that amount of time. From five weeks of age her baby slept through the night for twelve to thirteen hours. When the baby was four months old she began to wake him to nurse before she went to bed, because she felt that the long period without a feeding might force a return of menstruation. However, no bleeding occurred during those early months. Even though her baby did not nurse as frequently as mine or other babies, we figured that maybe our babies were spending about the same amount of time at the breast. Whereas my baby would nurse for about five to ten minutes at a feeding, her baby would nurse about twenty minutes at a feeding. Perhaps the time factor in a twenty-four-hour day wasn't as unequal as it at first appeared.

The attitudes of different doctors who saw this mother were interesting. The pediatrician saw no reason why this mother couldn't totally nurse her baby for nine months as long as the baby received some vitamin and iron drops. However, the obstetrician thought she was playing Vatican roulette and told her that she would be lucky if it worked. This doctor has told other nursing mothers that they should take other precautions or else he will be seeing them next year to deliver another baby. Mrs. C did not convince him; yet she relied on breast-feeding in spite of this doctor's opinions and in spite of her not wanting another pregnancy. Finally, at her last visit, the obstetrician said that he could see that it might work if a mother had a really aggressive baby— although this mother's baby was certainly not aggresive or very demanding at the breast.

Her general practitioner, on the other hand, was extremely interested in what she had to say and said he really learned something new. This doctor was very happy for her, said he would give the information to other interested patients, and also said he was especially pleased to see a healthy baby who was nursed so long on just mother's milk.

Mrs. C's baby looks as if she will wean herself by her first birthday. The mother is enjoying this relationship too much to stop the nursing abruptly, as she had originally planned.

MOTHER D

Mrs. D nursed her third baby completely for seven and a half months. The baby was eleven months old when menstruation returned. The mother weaned the baby at sixteen months of age.

This mother introduced cereal a week before having learned about the spacing benefit of total breast-feeding. She called her pediatrician and he told her it would be all right to drop the cereal and to completely nurse the baby.

In Mrs. D's own words she says: "Most of all, the child spacing and 100 percent nursing were the greatest helps." She had nursed her other two babies, but found that with this baby she had a very different and special relationship due simply to the complete breast-feeding. "I think 100 percent breast-feeding is the only way to start a baby out in this complex world of ours. For me it was the most wonderful experience of motherhood I have ever had."

AUTHOR'S EXPERIENCE

I wish I could say that someone had given me adequate instruction about breast-feeding with our first child, but the fact is that like most mothers I was really quite unknowledgeable about it. As a result, our first baby was never totally breast-fed. However, a bottle was a relatively infrequent thing for the first three months. I introduced juices at three months and solids at five months. My first period occurred at three months due to early weaning. I thought at the time that this was a natural occurrence, since my obstetrician told me I would have a period within three months following delivery regardless of how I fed the baby. Little did I realize until later how "un-natural" this occurrence was if you take nature as your norm. In addition, the use of the bottle

134

did interfere with lactation; I can remember my husband often encouraging me to let the baby suck so I would have more milk instead of relying more and more on the bottle.

After our second baby was born I had picked up considerably more information about total breast-feeding. As a result, I introduced solids when our baby was nearing the end of her eighth month. The weaning proceeded gradually and my periods started four months later. While nursing this baby, I was also encouraged by the fact that I knew two mothers who completely nursed their babies while I was doing so. One of the mothers was Mrs. A, mentioned previously; the other mother nursed completely for nine months, and menstruation returned when her baby was about eighteen months old. She was still nursing and giving night feedings at this age. Menstruation for all three of us did not resume until our babies were twelve to eighteen months old.

When I informed our pediatrician of my plans, he was most interested, since he admitted not knowing anything about it. During our visits he never once made a reference to solids or juices. When the baby rejected the vitamin drops, he said that they were not that important but that I should make sure my diet was good. He checked her iron before and again after she reached six months and found everything satisfactory. Most of all, he was pleased with her health and good disposition.

I admired this particular doctor—not only for his medical knowledge and interest in breast-feeding—but for a special reason: he respected my right in deciding at what time I should offer my baby something else besides breast milk. I hinted, and even asked for his opinion as to when I should begin solids. He never answered that question. Neither he nor my husband would offer an opinion, other than letting me know I was free to go as long as I desired and as long as the baby continued to thrive on breast milk. The decision was thus entirely mine. At eight months, our baby showed her first tooth, so I took this eruption to mean a time for weaning. At least it became the answer to my question, "How long?" However, if the tooth had erupted at four or six months of age, I would have ignored this sign; if the baby were unhappy and needed the solids, I would have begun solids earlier. The introduction of solids at such a late date in no way detracted from her health or disposition. Only her mother was the wiser when people commented on how well she must eat or asked if she was that good all the time.

Our girl thus became familiar with nonmilk foods and took a sip occasionally from a cup. I continued to offer the breast so that she was still receiving most of her liquid diet from me. At age eighteen months she came down with a cold, and I took advantage of the opportunity to wean her. That type of weaning is inconsistent with what I recommend in this book, and I would do it differently today.

Our third baby was born when our second was twenty-four months old. She was also nursed completely for eight months, at which time she began taking solids. Menstruation returned to me at ten and a half months—exactly fourteen days after she had a slight illness. During the illness she had a good disposition but a large decrease in appetite for any food, including breast milk. For two days this reduction in the amount of sucking caused, I feel, a premature return of menstruation. She weaned several months prior to her fourth birthday.

My experience duplicates that of the other four cases as regards the natural spacing of births, and reinforces what I have learned from the literature. That is, at the same time that total breast-feeding supplies the finest nutrition and provides the atmosphere for a rich emotional development, it likewise suppresses ovulation and provides for the natural spacing of births. In the past four years I have had two pregnancies, which accounted for about eighteen months of amenorrhea. In that same amount of time, I had twenty-two months of amenorrhea due to breast-feeding. I have thus had more months of infertility through breast-feeding than through pregnancy.

12

The Mail Box

Mothers who have written me after reading the first version of this book have three themes running through their letters: (1) they lack support from doctors and relatives; (2) they are deeply appreciative for the information and support given by La Leche League; (3) they experienced longer amenorrhea by following the natural plan for mothering.

These mothers wrote from the United States, Canada, Australia, and New Zealand. Here are some excerpts from a few letters expressing their thoughts and experiences on the subject of natural spacing and mothering. I am including them because many mothers find support in knowing about the experiences of others.

"God didn't mean for women to become 'baby-factories,' giving birth to a new child every year. In order that our bodies could recuperate from childbirth and build up strength for a next pregnancy, He planned that breast-feeding would render us infertile for one to two years. Why should we bother with foams, artificial devices or the pill? God's plan is so much nicer!"

"You may also wonder if I am of a faith that does not condone birth control means. No, I am not, and I have in fact taken the pill for a year and a half between my two children. My boys are over three years apart, as I remained sterile for nearly a year after those pills. So I've found breast-feeding a lovely blessing in every way, and the infertility is only a convenient side effect.

137

We've decided on a third child at the earliest possible date—considering the breast-feeding situation, of course."

"I'd just like to say I feel certain breast-feeding has a very definite effect on child spacing. With my other, bottle-fed children I conceived again at eight months after delivery, despite other contraceptives. So far it has been fifteen months since the last baby was born. No period yet."

"I first read your book when Lynda had nearly weaned herself. It certainly makes sense, and I am looking forward to having another baby. I only wish I had known more when Lynda was a baby because contraception can be such a worry. I would *never* go on the pill again."

"Our number one baby was twenty months old when number two was born. Our number two was thirty-four months old when number three was born. I nursed numbers one and two for about one year together. A lot of people have questioned me—'Is that all you're doing?' I tell them I have faith. It has worked for us and I really believe in it."

"My husband and I are very pleased with this most natural means of spacing children. It is especially great these hectic months after birth, when tension over effectiveness of other means and adjustments to a new baby can put a strain on a marriage. We feel this way is best for our family in every way and are overjoyed it works so well."

"Our fifteen-month-old is still nursing three or four times a day. For a while it seemed he wasn't too interested, except early in the morning. I haven't had a period yet. The other day someone was complaining of cramps and discomfort with her period and I mentioned that since my first baby I have never had all that cramping and pain with my periods. Then I said, 'But come to think of it, I've had so few periods.' And my friend said, 'You know, you are the truly liberated woman!' How true! So far I will have had eleven periods in over eight years. This is with three babies."

138

"I just finished reading your book. Very informative! I just wish I could have read it twenty years ago! Our little girl wakes at night to be nursed and sometimes nurses often at night. We have a king-size bed so it really doesn't bother our sleep. We have relied totally on nursing for preventing a new pregnancy. It is the most enjoyable method of spacing babies. I just regret all the years that were completely safe or could have been and we didn't know it."

"As a Protestant, it had never been presented to my husband and I as a logical way to have a family. Our sweet little one is nine days old, and she will be the first one not to have a soother. Many of my acquaintances are put right on the IUD after their first baby and I think it's a shame when God intended His way of spacing little ones."

"This is the only method of child spacing that appeals to my husband and me in every possible way. Myself, I look for simpler answers—ones that women in nontechnological societies might discover—and in breast-feeding I found it."

"Perhaps the future of the family is at stake in this generation, but I have faith in God that perhaps some of the turmoil the world is going through will make us return to the warmth and love, the heartaches and the pride that can come from close family unity. Developing as human beings is the only thing that can have meaning in a world that so often labels us as numbers. Breast-feeding and natural family planning can give us direction as families by turning us toward humanness."

"My second child is now seven and a half months old. I haven't had a period yet. I totally breast-fed him until six and a half months, when he wanted food from my plate. I learned from experience that I must be careful about introducing solids. My baby nurses twice at night and for long periods of time."

"When my doctor spoke to me in the hospital, he was pleased I was going to nurse and asked that I not give solids until at least a month. I said: 'Great, I wasn't intending to introduce them for four months or more.' He said: 'I fully approve, but I think you

had better be-
gin with some cereal
or other iron food around
four months or have a
blood check.' That's a pediatrician I like! He also
said he usually has to fight
his mothers and gives in
at one month for solids.

Nursing Lisa has been a beautiful experience. She is a wonderful, contented baby. Her weight gain has been well above normal and her iron level measured at six months was fine. She gave up that 2:00 A.M. feed very early at about six weeks. At three months she gave up the 10:00 P.M. feed, so I had that long stretch without nursing at night again. I went back to night feedings but she gave up one of her daytime feedings so I was still on four feeds a day. I spasmodically fed her at night but it was obvious she did not want it, so I finally gave up and she seemed happier. At six months she went to three feeds a day with four every now and then. I began solids around five and a half months with small pieces of banana and gradually introduced other foods. Lisa was really ready for solids and took to them greedily. I always nursed her before solids. Now she eats three meals a day and I cut out her mid-day nursing. However, she has been sick the last three nights with high fever and she has gone back to nursing as nothing else makes her happy. One would expect a return of periods and/or ovulation with decrease in nursing, but apparently I must be able to keep the levels of 'inhibitory hormone' high enough to prevent ovulation."

"My brother-in-law goes to Peru each summer and he has done a little investigating about the nursing habits of the Indians. In rural areas they nurse for three or more years and he never saw the mothers offering their young liquid from a cup. He assumed the child at some time or other learned this completely by himself."

"We now know why breast-feeding spaces babies—the baby is always in our bed to nurse at night!"

"I read a book written by an elderly lady from North Carolina describing life there in the latter half of the nineteenth century. She said the baby spent the day in the cradle and nights in bed with his parents. Babies were never allowed to cry."

"It has been my observation in three years of talking to nursing mothers, that night feedings are a critical factor in extending the time of postpartum amenorrhea, and that taking the baby to bed with you is a critical factor in extending night feedings. May I make a suggestion? It helps to stop thinking in terms of the bedroom and consider a sleeping room, with safe, low mattresses where the baby always sleeps. Then supplement this with a nearby, comfortable area to which the husband and wife may retire if they wish privacy. Many of the 'overwhelming problems' of breast-feeding are really problems of logistics—confining floor plans, furniture, clothes, etc., which dictate a life style that conflicts with breast-feeding."

"Not much has been written about the nursing mother who must return to work, perhaps because most people view the combination of nursing with outside employment as a most unlikely one. I find breast-feeding very meaningful under the circumstances. It assures the baby of getting the attention he needs under even the most hectic circumstances. Our breast-fed baby is outgoing and good humored despite Mommy's job, and our three-year-old is moody and demands constant reassurance though I did not work until she was three. This contribution of breast-feeding to a well-balanced personality does not receive nearly as much credit as it is due. Breast-feeding also helps a working mother by giving her confidence that she is providing her best for her child though she cannot always be near him. There are difficulties such as leaking and keeping up the milk supply, but the first requirement is nursing as frequently and as long as the circumstances permit."

"My husband gave me much support with this breast-feeding experience. It was his total lack of it with our first child that made me give it up the day we came home from the hospital, plus my own ignorance. The sight of a nursing infant turned his stomach at that time. This was one of the reasons I never attempted to nurse the second child. However, through the material made available to me from LLLI, both my husband and I grew more knowledgeable about breast-feeding. Now he feels sorry for babies who have to take a bottle. He feels, as I do, that the poor little ones are being denied the best start in life available to them."

"This was the first baby totally breast-fed for six months, and also a true baby-led weaning. The assurance I got from my husband was what I needed. He really acted as a buffer against the relatives and friends. My doctor was a tremendous help by his positive attitude. It also helped to be able to quote his remarks to the relatives. [The baby] nursed very infrequently, but gained three pounds every month for the first six months except one month he gained four pounds. I am currently nursing our seventeen-month-old baby without a return of my periods."

"Baby sucked her fingers a lot the first three months when I tried halfheartedly to follow a schedule. She stopped when I really relaxed and fed her as often and as long as she needed."

"We never 'started' Meghan on solids, just let her help herself to whatever suitable finger foods might be within reach. I don't think she had anything until about nine months, and then she surely went slow and easy. She would never tolerate anyone coming at her with a spoon or fork, although when interested she could use them herself very well. Most of her nutrition *still* comes from me, and some days she eats very little if anything. Other days she will go on a binge and eat *a lot* of something or other. She is healthy and solid and a live wire and adorable. She never had a cup or a glass either until way past a year, when she would climb out onto the table to get one, or snatch one out of your hands."

"We went through a terrible round of stomach flu with our whole family terribly ill for a full week. We, including myself, ran temperatures as high as 104 with vomiting and diarrhea. I was too sick to get up, but my baby slept right with me and nursed whenever he desired. He never showed any signs whatsoever of contracting the sickness."

"Our fourth baby was born at home because we wanted no interference with hospital schedules. Because of this we nursed almost continually from a few minutes after birth until she was twenty-five hours old. The only times she wasn't at breast were when I was otherwise occupied—i.e., changing pads. This was beautiful for both of us. My milk was in at sixteen hours and she passed all the black stool by two days of age. She (six and a half months old) is now having one meal of solids per day. This is mainly meat, a few ounces of our regular table food. She has never slept in a bed other than ours since birth. She nurses on and off during the night, but I really don't know how often. I sleep nude from the waist up, so does the baby, in order to allow more skin contact. Consequently she eats whenever she likes. We use no other form of birth control so I imagine our next baby will come along in two years. My husband and I are both enjoying this fourth baby. It's my husband's idea to have her sleep with us. He feels she will benefit greatly by the close cuddling she gets at night. With three other children to care for, he feels the baby may not get enough holding and loving during the day. Therefore, he wants to ensure her getting her share of me at night."

"I believe not only in lying down while nursing but also in sleeping with one's children. My son nursed on and off through all of his nights. He is twenty-two months old and I have not yet had a period. Sleeping with one's children is so easy, so natural, so safe, so warm and loving."

"Baby number two and I are having a delightfully close time together. It is true that I rather regret not having been as well-informed for our first baby; however, the warm mothering feelings that this approach to nursing engenders spills over to him and he is caught in the glow of this mother-baby relationship. I am going to try baby-led weaning and am most blessed in a very supportive philosopher-husband whose knowledge of rational psychology helps us define what is human."

"I really feel that my husband has been the mainstay of my success. I always wanted to nurse but lacked the courage of my convictions. Many times when I felt I should start solids or encourage weaning, my husband would say 'Let's wait a day or two.' Our next child, which I hope to conceive soon, will never know what a rubber nipple is!"

"Brian was two in December and still nurses *very* frequently. I really do enjoy being able to be near him this way and it's great for naps and bedtime. He really demands to nurse if I don't offer and if I try to distract him he gets too upset. The reason I tried to cut down on the nursings is that we believe a new baby may be coming. I do not want to have to wean Brian and would not mind nursing both after the baby comes. My doctor saw a friend recently who was also in a similar situation and he told her to wean immediately, that it would harm the fetus. She hasn't been able to stop nursing her seventeen-month-old either. I need information to convince my doctor otherwise or else I'm going to change doctors. I wonder if I could find one who would approve. They hardly know about nursing *one,* but while pregnant, I don't know? And nursing two? Wow!"

"Our doctor is very supportive of breast-feeding, yet he has not seen a nursing baby as old as my twenty-month-old. He is now becoming very negative. She should be weaned and is not gaining enough. He is quite horrified of the possibility of my nursing through a pregnancy and nursing both. He recommended radical weaning now. This has become a source of contention between us. I have no intentions of following his wishes."

"Our two-year-old weaned himself recently. The first time he quit for a month; then he resumed for another month and now he has given it up again. I'm glad he did the deciding. It really makes me feel right inside. I know you know the joys of nursing a toddler, but this is the first time for me and it was so rewarding, so special. I do think God was very wise in his plan for babies and mothers. I'm wondering if perhaps the nursing experience doesn't help the weaning that must come when the young adult leaves home."

"My youngest is now four years old and weaned about a week before his fourth birthday. He still has a little try once in a while but informs me I'm empty. I have enjoyed baby-led weaning so much and can see all the advantages so clearly. I only wish I'd been doing this with the first two, although they are reaping the benefits, too. I can't think of anything that's more enjoyable and rewarding than being a mother."

"Nursing an older baby seemed to be a particular experience with me as Lennie didn't wean until she was three. Now my arms are so empty! I find much joy in the children as they are growing and maturing, but there is just that special *something* about breast-feeding that we don't ever experience again."

Appendix I

A Review of the Research

The following material summarizes most of the work that has been conducted on the subject of breast-feeding and infertility. This review has its limitations. In the first place, when breast-feeding was the accepted norm, say before 1920, medical research was not as well developed as it is today. On the other hand, as medical research became more popular, breast-feeding became less and less popular and therefore became less a subject of research. Furthermore, while research that might have been done before 1920 may have dealt with mothers who were breast-feeding 100 percent or totally for a considerable length of time, present research is hampered by the fact that women who are included in a sample of nursing mothers are usually not nursing 100 percent. Many are using the bottle or solids. Sometimes the researcher does not clearly define how the mother is feeding the baby. Breast-feeding, then, is difficult to study in a culture where so few mothers nurse for a considerable length of time, and where artificial feeding of the infant is a common practice.

Research today becomes more difficult due to the heavy emphasis placed on contraceptive practices. The researcher should know the personal views of each mother to be certain that breast-feeding is the only method of family planning used for a certain period of time. In our country it is interesting to note that, regardless of our emphasis on bottles, early solids, and contraceptive practices, the studies show that breast-feeding still decreases the fertility rates. They also show that breast-feeding can be a very effective and natural way to space babies.

Sucking

This review attempts to show the important role sucking plays in the maintenance of natural infertility. Hormones cannot be ignored in the total picture. However, since so little is known about the complex hormonal pattern involved in the maintenance of lactation infertility, no explanation will be attempted. The discussion instead will center around the sucking act—an external act we can see and understand, unlike the hormones themselves.

How does the sucking of an infant at the breast of his mother influence menstruation and ovulation? The following selections were taken from studies that sought to explain the absence of menstruation during lactation.

In 1951 Dr. Albert Sharman, of the Royal Samaritan Hospital for Women in Glasgow, noticed that menstruation occurred during lactation for some mothers and not for others. From this observation the doctor felt that lactation alone did not prevent a woman from having periods, but that there would have to be some other contributory cause.[1]

In 1954 a research team concluded from their work that the reappearance of the menstrual cycles in the early months after childbirth was normally brought about by a reduction in a suckling stimulus.[2] This reduction is voluntary, or else is brought about by the use of artificial foods to supplement the mother's milk.[3]

In 1967 another research team found that follicular growth (development necessary before ovulation can occur) and ovulation were inhibited during suckling.[4]

In 1949 Dr. Isadore Udesky of the Northwestern University Medical School and Michael Reese Hospital had reported the same observation from his studies. He added that suckling is directly responsible for this inhibition of the ovarian cycle.[5]

It is interesting to note an endocrine study that was done in 1967. Dr. C. E. Grosvenor and his associates found that two things were necessary for efficient release of prolactin in response to suckling among suckled mother rats: (1) The suckling had to be periodic and (2) it

1. Albert Sharman, "Ovulation After Pregnancy," *Fertility and Sterility* 2 (1951): 371.
2. "Suckling" and "sucking" are both used in the research terminology interchangeably. Sucking is a narrower term, referring only to the baby's act of sucking at the breast. Suckling is broader; sometimes it means the individual sucking acts; at other times, it refers to the breast-feeding process over a period of months.
3. Thomas McKeown and J. R. Gibson, "A Note on Menstruation and Conception During Lactation," *Journal of Obstetrics and Gynecology of the British Empire* 61 (1954): 824.
4. Hiroshi Minaguchi and Joseph Meites, "Effects of Suckling on Hypothalamic LH-Releasing Factor and Prolactin Inhibiting Factor, and on Pituitary LH and Prolactin," *Endocrinology* 80 (1967): 603.
5. Isadore Udesky, "Ovulation in Lactating Women," *American Journal of Obstetrics and Gynecology* 59 (1950): 843.

had to occur at short intervals.[6] Prolactin is one of the hormones said to be responsible for lactation. (I might add here that these quantitative characteristics of the sucking act—short intervals and periodic—also seem to influence the effectiveness of the spacing mechanism.)

In 1965 the World Health Organization reported that there are two obvious stimuli that interrupt the reproductive cycles in the adult female. These are coitus which results in pregnancy and suckling.[7] In another report the WHO said that with lactation (1) there is a period of time after delivery when a woman does not menstruate or ovulate, (2) the first period often occurs without ovulation, (3) infertility remains for a longer period if lactation is prolonged, and (4) our knowledge of lactation with respect to infertility is still incomplete.[8]

The Inactivity of Ovaries During Lactation

Studies also show that the ovaries are at rest or nonfunctioning during lactation. It was suggested in 1961 that the absence of menstruation during lactation is due to ovarian inactivity.[9]

In 1943 Dr. Paul Topkins concluded that the absence of menstruation during lactation is due to the suppression of the ovarian function. He stated that during lactation amenorrhea, the follicles in the ovaries failed to mature and rupture.[10]

When a doctor wrote to the *Journal of the American Medical Association* in 1958 asking why a woman does not become pregnant or ovulate when she is breast-feeding, the editor's reply was the following:

Ovarian function is suppressed but not completely inhibited during lactation. Recent evidence indicates that it is the stimulus of suckling of the infant rather than lactation which acts on the pituitary gland, probably by way of the midbrain. The decrease in the frequency of

6. C. E. Grosvenor, F. Mena, and D. A. Schaefgen, "Effect of Non-suckling Interval and Duration of Suckling on the Suckling-Induced Fall in Pituitary Prolactin Concentration in the Rat," *Endocrinology* 81 (1967): 449.

7. World Health Organization, "Neuroendocrinology and Reproduction in the Human," Technical Report Series no. 304 (Geneva, 1965).

8. World Health Organization, "Biology of Human Reproduction," Technical Report Series no. 280 (Geneva, 1964); *idem.,* "Physiology of Lactation," Technical Report Series no. 305 (Geneva, 1965).

9. W. C. Keettel and J. T. Bradbury, "Endocrine Studies of Lactation Amenorrhea," *American Journal of Obstetrics and Gynecology* 82 (1961): 995.

10. Paul Topkins, "The Histologic Appearance of the Endometrium During Lactation and Its Relationship to Ovarian Function," *American Journal of Obstetrics and Gynecology* 77 (1959): 921.

feedings and the cessation of nursing result in the reestablishment of ovarian function, the reappearance of menstruation, and, ultimately, ovulation. Complete breast-feeding in the early months of life is a fairly effective method of suppressing ovarian function and conception.[11]

Lactation and Conception

During the years 1938 to 1940, Dr. M. Robinson noted that pregnancies occurred while mothers were nursing their babies. The nursing mothers (number not given) conceived two to three months after delivery. The eleven hundred nursing cases in this study, however, were characterized by early weaning and "failing lactation" (the title of the research paper).[12] Since the study involved only cases of unsuccessful nursing and "premature weaning" according to Dr. Robinson, we might assume that the breast-feeding was not complete nor the milk supply ample at the time of conception.

In 1943 Dr. Paul Topkins observed that during the nonmenstrual phase among nursing mothers, conception rarely occurred. He questioned to what degree ovulation is inhibited among nursing mothers and performed 145 biopsies on 28 normal nursing mothers who had had regular menstrual cycles before delivery. Women who had 4 or more specimens taken were chosen for this study. Dr. Topkins concluded that ovulation is suppressed during lactation and that this inhibition of ovarian activity is complete when menstruation is absent and incomplete when menstruation is present.[13]

In 1946 Dr. J. W. B. Douglas of the University of London studied the different aspects of breast-feeding among 4,669 babies. Since in this study a breast-fed baby was considered breast-fed until he was entirely weaned off the breast, it is impossible to determine the duration of complete breast-feeding in these cases. Mothers in this study averaged about five and a half months of nursing.

One aspect that interested Dr. Douglas was the rate of pregnancies during the first year after childbirth among bottle-feeding and breast-feeding mothers. He found that during the first nine months after childbirth the number of pregnancies was considerably lower among those mothers who were nursing their babies, but that during the ten-

11. Paul Topkins, "Letters to the Editor," *Journal of the American Medical Association* 167 (1958): 144.
12. M. Robinson, "Failing Lactation," *Lancet* 1 (1943): 66.
13. *Op. cit.*

to twelve-month period the number of pregnancies was the same for both groups. He explained this conclusion by saying that in the latter months of this study mothers were only nursing their babies once or twice during the day. The doctor pointed out that it was impossible to determine two varying factors: the use of birth control and the frequency of coitus. However, he felt that the breast-feeding mothers were not practicing a more effective method of birth control because their fertility rate equaled that of the bottle-feeding mothers once breast-feeding ceased.[14]

In 1950 Dr. Isadore Udesky performed repeated endometrial biopsies on 121 nursing mothers during the nonmenstrual phase to determine any evidence of ovulation before menstruation returned. The doctor said that all of the nursing mothers were nursing "regularly." The question arises as to whether a nursing mother can become pregnant before menstruation returns following childbirth. He answered yes, but only in a very few—about 3½ percent. His primary conclusion was that, during lactation and the absence of menstruation, the suppression of the ovarian function is almost complete.[15]

In 1951 Dr. Albert Sharman presented a paper to the Seventh Annual Meeting of the American Society for the Study of Sterility outlining a follow-up study carried out on 834 women during the nine-month period following delivery. Dr. Sharman defines the type of feeding with reference to the liquid diet of the baby. Complete lactators (196) apparently were those who only offered the breast. No bottle would have been offered on a regular basis among these mothers, for he defines the next group of women as partial lactators (356), or those who eventually offered the breast and the bottle toward the end of the study. Nonlactators (282) were those who offered only the bottle. Out of the total 834 women, only twelve (approximately 1½ percent) became pregnant during the nine-month period following childbirth, and all twelve had at least two menstrual periods before conception took place. A significant factor is that none of the "lactators" became pregnant during this time. Three women who became pregnant while partially nursing had all introduced the bottle at least a month or more before conception took place. Dr. Sharman concluded that there is a considerably lower risk of conception among nursing mothers.[16]

In a subsequent paper, written in 1954, Dr. Sharman was primarily

14. J. W. B. Douglas, "The Extent of Breast Feeding in Great Britain in 1946, with Special Reference to the Health and Survival of Children," *Journal of Obstetrics and Gynecology of the British Empire* 57 (1950): 335.
15. *Op. cit.*
16. *Op. cit.*

interested in recording the menstrual periods of apparently these same 834 women. His recordings and tables indicated that menstruation did occur at a later date among the nursing mothers.[17]

In 1953 a study was conducted by a registered nurse, Rose Gioiosa, at the Catholic Maternity Institute in Sante Fe, New Mexico, where encouragement and instruction are offered to nursing mothers. Among the 148 nursing mothers selected, 500 pregnancies were studied during the years. Only 46 of the 500 pregnancies occurred during the time of lactation, and these occurred during the weaning process in the latter months of breast-feeding. All other pregnancies occurred after the mothers had stopped nursing. The return of menstruation was not considered in this study.

From this study the nurse concluded that breast-feeding is a natural means of spacing children and that this protection lasts for about nine months or more, providing no formula is given to the baby. She emphasized that early solids or early supplements decreased the amount of time in which a mother is unable to conceive. The natural-spacing mechanism is shortened by early weaning, and as a result the mother conceives at a much earlier date than she would if she had nursed her baby for nine months or more without the use of bottles and had introduced supplementary solids only at about six months of age. She also strongly emphasized the need for educational programs to inform the youth and expectant parents of the advantages of breast-feeding and especially of natural spacing.[18]

Rose Gioiosa also wrote another article, "Breastfeeding and Child Spacing,"[19] in which she showed that one of the most practical advantages of breast-feeding is that a mother can space babies naturally, that she does not need to use any other family-planning technique in order to space her children. She related doctors' experiences in other countries, where they found that mothers nurse for a long time because they believe that breast-feeding prevents the risk of another pregnancy. In certain countries (Africa, Ceylon, India, Iraq, Malaya, Syria) there are still places where breast-feeding is valued as a baby-spacer. She then analyzed the 1961 La Leche League Nationwide Survey and found once again that early weaning shortens the natural spacing interval afforded by breast-feeding.

In 1954 McKeown and Gibson studied 1,227 women for one year

17. Albert Sharman, "Menstruation after Childbirth," *Journal of Obstetrics and Gynecology of the British Empire* 58 (1954): 440.

18. Rose Gioiosa, "Incidence of Pregnancy During Lactation in 500 Cases," *American Journal of Obstetrics and Gynecology* 70 (1955): 162.

19. La Leche League reprint no. 121 (no longer available).

following childbirth. Of these mothers, 87 (7 percent) conceived during the year. No mother conceived while fully breast-feeding and before having periods. Two mothers who were nursing fully conceived after having one menstrual period. All the other mothers were using artificial feedings before conception occurred.[20]

In 1968 Dr. T. J. Cronin studied the basal temperature recordings of 174 mothers during the three months following childbirth. Among this group there were 93 who did not try to nurse their babies. For the mothers who did not nurse, the mean time up to the return of menstruation was 58.9 days, and the mean time up to the time of the first ovulation was 73.5 days after delivery.

There were twenty-eight mothers who stopped nursing less than four weeks after delivery. In this small group the doctor found that menstruation returned on the average 15.4 days earlier than it had for the nonnursing group. Yet these mothers who quit nursing at an early date had a mean period of 70.7 days before ovulation returned, a median figure which is very close to the nonnursing group.

Of the remaining fifty-three mothers who were still nursing after the twenty-eight-day period following childbirth, ten ovulated before the three-month period date following delivery. Five of the mothers already had a return of menstruation, four had stopped nursing at the time of ovulation, and only one nursing mother ovulated before the return of her menstrual periods. Ovulation in her case occurred at day seventy-three; menstruation appeared on day eighty-four; and she supplemented on day ninety-nine.

Observing other studies that had been done to determine the time of ovulation following childbirth and observing his own group of nursing mothers (many of whom supplemented in the early months or who stopped nursing during the three-month period following delivery), Dr. Cronin concluded that ovulation rarely occurs during the ten weeks following childbirth if the mother is fully nursing and if menstruation is not present.[21]

In 1933 Dr. C. H. Peckham from the Department of Obstetrics at Johns Hopkins University and Hospital analyzed Dr. Williams's study conducted on 2,885 women. Almost all of these mothers were nursing when they left the hospital, and most continued to nurse even if they used the bottle. Fifty percent of the mothers were still nursing at six months; 28 percent were still nursing at the end of the year. The aver-

20. *Op. cit.*
21. T. J. Cronin, "The Influence of Lactation upon Ovulation," *Lancet* 2 (1968): 422.

age duration of breast-feeding for this group was about eight and one-half months.

Of these 2,885 women, 30 percent conceived during the first year (about 877). Of the mothers who were nursing at the time of conception, over 50 percent menstruated four or more times before conception, but 10 percent conceived without menstruating.[22]

An Egyptian medical team studied the lactation patterns of 120 mothers by verbal questioning. The duration of breast-feeding among these women averaged 15.1 months. This study I found confusing; definitions were not clear. One-third of the mothers menstruated during the first three postpartum months and two-thirds during the first nine postpartum months with "full lactation" averaging nine months among these mothers. The incidence of pregnancy for nursing mothers during amenorrhea was given as 50 percent and during menstruation as 63 percent. The 50 percent risk factor during lactation amenorrhea is a much higher figure than those given in other studies. The doctors concluded that breast-feeding is an unsatisfactory method of birth control.[23]

In France Juliette Pascal studied the postpartum periods among nursing and nonnursing mothers for three years (1965–1968). Here are some of the conclusions: (1) The 449 nursing mothers averaged fifty-eight days of amenorrhea, although it is noted that menstruation returned most frequently in the forty- to forty-nine-day period following childbirth; (2) one-third of the nursing mothers run a risk of conceiving before the first postpartum menses; (3) only 3 percent run the risk of conception prior to the first postpartum menses if completely nursing.[24]

It is interesting that the first two conclusions might be what you would expect among bottle-feeding mothers. Suffice it to say that only 7 percent of these mothers nursed past six months and over half of them had quit nursing by the sixth week. An interesting comparison of Pascal's work and our survey is given later in the part of Appendix II dealing with the report on breast-feeding and amenorrhea by the author

22. C. H. Peckham, "An Investigation of Some Effects of Pregnancy Noted Six Weeks and One Year After Delivery," *Bulletin of the Johns Hopkins Hospital* 54 (1934): 186.

23. I. Kamal *et al.*, "Clinical, Biochemical, and Experimental Studies on Lactation," *American Journal of Obstetrics and Gynecology* 105 (1969): 314.

24. Juliette Pascal, "Some Aspects of Post-Partum Physiology" (Doctoral thesis presented at the University of Nancy, France, October 1969). Translation and summary by Dr. S. P. Carreau of Serena, Inc., and Dr. C. Lanctot of the Natural Family Planning Association of Connecticut.

and her husband. The primary reason for selecting Pascal's work for such a comparison was that this work was publicized among some natural family-planning groups as being a significant contribution.

Dr. Christopher Tietze of the Population Council sought to clarify the confusion as to whether or not a woman could conceive while nursing her baby and attempted to review all the available demographic medical work. In 1961 his work was presented before the International Population Conference; the paper was titled "The Effect of Breastfeeding on the Rate of Conception." In this paper he concluded the following points: (1) that the *prolonged* absence of menstruation seems to be the major factor involved in the delay of conception among nursing mothers; (2) that during breast-feeding, and with the absence of menstruation, "ovulation is suppressed and conception therefore impossible"; (3) that while ovulation is normally followed by a menstrual flow, "the first menstrual flow is preceded by ovulation in only a minority of [lactating] women"; (4) that a woman has about a 5 percent chance of conceiving before the return of her first menstrual period; (5) that when menstruation returns, the first two periods are usually infertile; (6) that the risk of conceiving "increases rapidly after menstruation has returned"; and (7) that since "breastfeeding tends to prolong the interval between pregnancies, it seems worthwhile to evaluate it as a method of child spacing."[25]

Dr. Konald Prem from the University of Minnesota Medical School is conducting a study on postpartum ovulation among nursing and non-nursing mothers with the aid of basal body temperature graphs. The nonnursing mother may experience ovulation as early as twenty-seven days after childbirth, and ovulation usually occurs prior to menses after a natural spontaneous abortion. The incidence of early return of fertility is great among nursing mothers who supplement or wean early, whereas the incidence of a fertile ovulation before menstruation during the first four to five months of total breast-feeding is small. Of the 118 nursing mothers, 6 conceived without a return of menstruation. Dr. Prem concluded that the risk of pregnancy during lactation amenorrhea is about 5 percent—1 percent less than the risk recorded by Remfry in 1895.[26]

25. Christopher Tietze, "The Effect of Breastfeeding on the Rate of Conception" (Paper presented at the International Population Conference, New York, September 1961), pp. 131–134.

26. Konald Prem, "Post-Partum Ovulation" (Paper presented at La Leche League International Convention, Chicago, July 1971).

The Duration of Amenorrhea

One table in Dr. Tietze's paper presented the works of various researchers, and here it was shown that in one group of 523 Indian women the mean duration of breast-feeding was sixteen and one-half months and the mean duration of amenorrhea was almost twelve months.[27]

In 1958, among a group of 272 nursing mothers in Bombay, it was found that a third of the mothers had a period by the ninth month, half of them had a period by the twelfth month, and for those who continued to nurse most did not have a return of menstruation until their baby was eighteen months old. Amenorrhea of a year or more was quite common in India—unlike the nursing mothers in America and in Europe. When menstruation did finally return after many months following childbirth, the research team observed that fertility was by no means impaired and conception was still possible. This is a normal condition and cannot be said to be pathological, for the authors said that once menstruation became reestablished, the fertility rate in these nursing mothers was as high as those for whom menstruation returned within the twelve-month period following childbirth.[28]

The effectiveness of the nonmenstrual phase in preventing pregnancy was studied among a group of 390 women and reported in the *Journal of Obstetrics and Gynecology of India*. The mean duration of lactation for 282 mothers was thirteen and one-half months; the mean duration of amenorrhea was five and one-quarter months. At the end of this study, the remaining 108 nursing mothers still had no return of their menstruation. The conclusions were that those who weaned early or used other milks early also had early menstruation; that the earlier artificial feeding began, the earlier menstruation began; and that menstruation began later among the fully lactating mothers.[29]

In Cairo a study of 145 nursing mothers found 86 of them experiencing amenorrhea. Among these 86, the duration of postpartum lactation amenorrhea ranged from six weeks to twenty-six months. Forty-

27. *Op. cit.*
28. H. Peters, S. Israel, and S. Purshottam, "Lactation Period in Indian Women—Duration of Amenorrhea and Vaginal and Cervical Cytology," *Fertility and Sterility* 9 (1958): 134; Paul Topkins, Abstract on "Peters, Israel, and Purshottam: Lactation Period in Indian Women: Duration of Amenorrhea and Vaginal and Cervical Cytology," *American Journal of Obstetrics and Gynecology* 77 (1959): 921.
29. Stuart Silverberg, "Selected Abstracts," *American Journal of Obstetrics and Gynecology* 82 (1961): 1196.

six mothers nursed for less than six months, 20 nursed from six to twelve months, and 20 nursed for a year or longer. Lactation amenorrhea lasted longer when the breast-feeding was not supplemented. The authors concluded that it is a fact that physiologic infertility is associated with postpartum lactation amenorrhea and should receive more attention as a result of population concerns.[30]

A study in Taiwan showed that the nursing mother averaged 10.6 months of amenorrhea as compared to 3.5 months of amenorrhea for the nonnursing mother. Thus, lactation provided on the average 7.1 more months of natural infertility. The researchers estimated that the prevalence of lactation with its additional 7.1 months of added infertility would prevent 20 percent of the births that would occur without lactation. They found that other factors influenced the duration of amenorrhea. Supplementation meant a shorter postpartum amenorrhea. In addition, city life and education reduced the period of lactation as well as the period of amenorrhea.[31]

While for some years it has been almost routine for some doctors to give a drug injection to most women after childbirth to dry up the milk supply, some new research is being done in the opposite direction. A medical team recently reported on their efforts to promote the production of breast milk and postpartum infertility through intravenous injections of thyrotropin-releasing hormone (TRH). They listed nausea, vomiting, urinary urgency, and breast engorgement as side effects, although their particular patients had only the latter.[32]

Such a drug may be helpful in the case where a mother wants to reestablish lactation, as for example, when wanting to nurse an adopted child or when an already weaned child needs breast milk. However, I hope that the use of such a drug will be confined to such rare cases and will not be used for birth-control purposes. All that the normal woman needs for an ample milk supply is a sucking baby from childbirth onwards.

In 1966 Dr. Eva J. Salber and her associates at the Harvard School of Public Health in Boston recorded the duration of amenorrhea after childbirth among 2,197 mothers. Nonnursing and nursing mothers had

30. M. F. El-Minawi and M. S. Foda, "Postpartum Lactation Amenorrhea," *American Journal of Obstetrics and Gynecology* 111 (September 1, 1971): 17.

31. A. Jain *et al.*, "Demographic Aspects of Lactation and Postpartum Amenorrhea," *Demography*, May 1970.

32. J. E. Tyson, H. G. Friesen, and M. S. Anderson, "Human Lactational and Ovarian Response to Endogenous Prolactin Release," *Science*, September 1972.

an overall mean period of 68 days without menstruation. Of the bottle-feeding mothers, 91 percent had a return of menstruation within three months after childbirth. The other 9 percent had a return within the next three months. On the other hand, 26 percent of the nursing mothers had a return of menses three months after childbirth, and about 60 percent had a return by six months postpartum. Most nursing mothers (95 percent) had a return of their period within six weeks after they discontinued nursing.[33]

These figures resemble those given by McKeown and Gibson in 1954. They found that 40 percent of the breast-feeding mothers and 95 percent of the bottle-feeding mothers had a return of menses four months after childbirth.[34]

On the other hand, Prem found in his study of seventy-four mothers who nursed longer than six months that fifty-seven (77 percent) were without menses at six months postpartum. Of those fifty-one mothers who breast-fed longer than nine months, thirty-one (61 percent) were without menses by nine months postpartum. He found that the return of menstruation occurred most frequently in the nine- to twelve-month period following childbirth. Many of the mothers in this study were associated with La Leche League, which encourages total breast-feeding in the early months of life, and this probably accounts for the longer duration of amenorrhea in Dr. Prem's study.[35]

In our survey we found that those women who totally breast-fed for at least five months averaged 11.6 months without menses and that the return of menstruation occurred most frequently in the nine- to twelve-month period following childbirth. Of those mothers who followed the natural mothering program the average duration of amenorrhea was 14.6 months and the greatest frequency of menses return occurred in the thirteen- to sixteen-month period following childbirth.[36]

Infertile Periods

Inés de Allende of Argentina made a thorough review of the research that had been done to determine whether or not a woman could have a menstrual period without having ovulated beforehand. From his

33. E. Salber, M. Feinleib, and B. Macmahon "The Duration of Post-partum Amenorrhea," *American Journal of Epidemiology* 82 (1966): 347.
34. *Op. cit.*
35. *Op. cit.*
36. S. Kippley and J. Kippley, "Report on Breastfeeding and Amen-orrhea," *Marriage and Family Newsletter*, March 1972. Later published in a revised form as "The Relation Between Breastfeeding and Amenorrhea: Report of a Survey" in the *Journal of Obstetrical, Gynecological and Neonatal Nursing* 1 (November–December 1972): 15.

investigation he found that these infertile periods were first suggested in the 1920s by Corner as a result of his studies on the monkey. Corner's belief was soon proven to be fact in the 1930s by three different research projects; all three projects carried out their diagnostic procedures on the human female.

In 1956 de Allende reported from his own work and that of others that (1) infertile periods occur occasionally even in the healthy, non-pregnant, nonnursing mother during the full sexual activity period, (2) that rarely does a woman have only fertile periods, and (3) that there are more infertile periods in proportion to fertile periods at the beginning and at the end of a woman's reproductive life.[37]

In 1938 Dr. Paul Lass and his associates from the Department of Obstetrics and Gynecology and Biochemistry of the College of Physicians and Surgeons at Columbia University, New York City, carried out a study on forty-seven menstruating mothers in which regular monthly periods were observed for a nine-month period following childbirth. These women who were not nursing their babies completely (weaning occurred during the time of the study) and who were having regular menstrual cycles had 55 percent of those periods recorded as infertile. One mother, on the other hand, who nursed every four hours had all infertile periods (eight in number) before weaning was completed. After cessation of breast-feeding, her menstrual cycles were fertile. The first menstrual periods in this study were experienced thirty to one hundred days after childbirth.[38] The duration of amenorrhea among these mothers was equivalent in length to the expectant norm of nonnursing mothers following childbirth.

In 1950 Dr. Isadore Udesky from Northwestern University Medical School and Michael Reese Hospital studied one group of thirty-six mothers who had their first periods while nursing. He found that 14 percent of these women gave evidence of ovulation either preceding or "from twenty days on" after the first period; over 28 percent of the periods after the third period occurred with ovulation during lactation.

On the other hand, in the same study there were also two hundred endometrial biopsies taken on another group of eighty-five normal nursing mothers who had no return of menses. Of these biopsies, 98.5 percent were infertile in character and 1.5 percent (three mothers) were fertile in character. In each of the three cases menstruation followed. Udesky also referred to a 1937 study by Rock and Bartlett that answered the question of whether a woman can become pregnant

37. Inés de Allende, "Anovulatory Cycles in Women," *American Journal of Anatomy* 98 (1956): 293.

38. P. Lass, J. Smelser, and R. Kurzrok, "Studies Relating To Time of Human Ovulation: III During Lactation," *Endocrinology* 23 (1938): 39.

during lactation amenorrhea by saying that it was possible in "about 3.5 percent of cases where the first ovulation is followed immediately by conception."

Dr. Udesky's paper was presented at the Chicago Gynecological Society in 1949. After his presentation several doctors had these points to offer during the discussion period that followed:

1. Dr. George W. Bartelmez, who has himself done studies on the human uterus during menstruation, pointed out that there is a possible error that one will diagnose too many fertile periods during lactation that are actually infertile, since Dr. Udesky's work and Dr. Hartman's work show us that the change from the atypical or infertile to the typical or fertile state is a very gradual change. (This point of diagnosing too many ovulations, I might add here, was also determined to be true by de Allende when using the basal temperature method. He found that about a third of the cycles [49 of 155 periods] that were recorded as fertile according to the basal temperature method were infertile according to the vaginal smear tests.)[39]

2. Dr. M. Edward Davis said that Dr. Scheitema and he carried out a study in 1942 to determine ovarian activity after delivery among nonnursing mothers. His endometrial biopsies revealed that ovulation rarely occurred before the first menstrual period, that ovulation occurred in about 50 percent of the second periods, and that ovulation was associated with nearly all of the third periods. The two doctors concluded that this gradual pattern from the fertile to the infertile or from the infertile to the fertile condition in the adult female was witnessed at the beginning of the menstrual cycles in early life, at the end of the menstrual cycles in later life, and also at the return of the menstrual cycles following childbirth.

Dr. Udesky closed the discussion period by saying that ovulation is more likely to occur during the weaning process and that this is why doctors know of mothers who have conceived while nursing their babies.[40]

Dr. Albert Sharman carried out a study on eighty-five menstruating mothers from a period of five days to nine months following childbirth. Of these eighty-five, sixty-eight were nonnursing mothers and fourteen were nursing mothers throughout the duration of the study. The number of nursing mothers was small, since most mothers stopped nursing before menstruation returned. First biopsies showed that eleven (79 percent) of the fourteen nursing mothers were in an

39. *Op. cit.*
40. *Op. cit.*

infertile condition and three (21 percent) were in a fertile condition. On the other hand, about 71 percent of the nonnursing mothers were shown to be in a fertile condition. Dr. Sharman concluded that breast-feeding does tend to retard the return of ovulation.[41]

Natural Spacing

During the 1950s Dr. Otto Schaefer noted that with traditional nursing among the Eskimos the next baby arrived about three years later. He concluded that the traditionally small-sized Eskimo family was due to prolonged nursing more than high infant mortality. In fact, in another study done by his Canadian Medical Service between 1962 and 1965, it was found that infant mortality was always higher among bottle-fed infants. In addition, the bottle-fed children had more gastrointestinal diseases, respiratory and middle-ear diseases, and more anemia.

Dr. Schaefer observed that the rapid introduction of bottles from the trading posts changed feeding habits and fertility patterns drastically. The birthrate jumped 50 percent, from less than forty births per thousand in the mid-1950s to sixty-four per thousand ten years later. The closer the Eskimo families lived to the trading posts, the more frequently their babies arrived. He mentioned that in the last twenty years the Eskimos have had a population explosion as great or greater than that experienced by any other developing nation. This explosion is "due less to the reduction in infant mortality than to the jump in birthrate"; the increased birthrate is attributed to bottle-feeding and a shortened lactation period. This factor, he claimed, is overlooked when studying the population problem in other countries.[42]

In 1960 and 1971 Dr. J. A. Hildes and Dr. Schaefer conducted studies on the Igloolik Eskimos. One outstanding observation dealt with the difference in the fertility rates among the older women as opposed to the younger women. Women aged thirty to fifty years who had traditionally breast-fed for two to three years conceived twenty to thirty months after childbirth, whereas the younger mothers under thirty years of age who bottle-fed conceived two to four months after childbirth. These doctors noted that other researchers attribute the population explosion in other countries to a reduced mortality rate. However, the Ig_looliks have a population problem in spite of their high infant death rate. The doctors found that it is the rapid

41. Sharman, "Ovulation After Pregnancy."
42. Otto Schaefer, "When the Eskimo Comes to Town," *Nutrition Today*, November–December 1971, pp. 15–16.

urbanization of these Eskimos during the past twenty years that is responsible for the increase in births, urbanization that brought rapid communication, and thus a rapid introduction of the baby bottle, to these people. Thus they lost the natural population control that prolonged breast-feeding had previously given them.[43]

This review and most of the material written on breast-feeding and amenorrhea or the rate of conception fail to describe clearly the type of breast-feeding or mothering involved. In spite of this fact, it becomes fairly obvious that breast-feeding plays an important role in postpartum infertility and can influence the birthrate of an individual family as well as a nation.

43. J. A. Hildes and O. Schaefer, "Health of Igloolik Eskimos and Changes with Urbanization" (Paper presented at the Circumpolar Health Symposium, Oulu, Finland, June 1971).

Appendix II

The Relation Between Breast-feeding and Amenorrhea: Report of a Survey

Sheila K. Kippley, B.S., and John F. Kippley, M.A., M.A.T.

In several studies of the relation between breast-feeding and the infertility it induces, the observation has been made that supplementary feedings reduce infertility.[1] Other studies[2] have revealed a vast difference between the breast-feeding–amenorrhea experience of Asian-Indian women and women of the North American–European culture. Peters, Israel, and Purshottam[3] showed that lactation amenorrhea of a year was quite common among Indian women, while Pascal[4] studied a French group whose lactation amenorrhea averaged only fifty-eight days. Salber, Feinleib, and Macmahon[5] showed that in more than 60

1. F. Rice, "The Function of Lactation," *The Family Today* (Washington, D.C.: Family Life Bureau, National Catholic Welfare Council, 1944), pp. 96–100; Rose Gioiosa, "Incidence of Pregnancy in Lactation in 500 Cases," *American Journal of Obstetrics and Gynecology* 70 (1955): 162; T. J. Cronin, "The Influence of Lactation upon Ovulation," *Lancet* 2 (1968): 422.

2. Christopher Tietze, "The Effect of Breastfeeding on the Rate of Conception" (Paper presented at the International Population Conference, New York, September 1961); H. Peters, S. Israel, and S. Purshottam, "Lactation Period in Indian Women–Duration of Amenorrhea and Vaginal and Cervical Cytology," *Fertility and Sterility* 9 (1958): 134; Stuart Silverberg, "Selected Abstracts," *American Journal of Obstetrics and Gynecology* 82 (1961): 1196.

3. H. Peters, S. Israel, and S. Purshottam, "Lactation Period in Indian Women—Duration of Amenorrhea and Vaginal and Cervical Cytology," *Fertility and Sterility* 9 (1958).

4. Juliette Pascal, "Some Aspects of Post-Partum Physiology" (Doctoral thesis presented at the University of Nancy, France, October 1969). Translation and summary by Dr. S. P. Carreau of Serena, Inc., and Dr. C. Lanctot of the Natural Planning Association of Connecticut.

5. E. Salber, M. Feinleib, and B. Macmahon, "The Duration of Postpartum Amenorrhea," *American Journal of Epidemiology* 82 (1966): 347.

percent of mothers who nursed for six months menses returned by six months. Gioiosa's analysis[6] of a La Leche League survey indicated that the early introduction of formulas and other foods reduced infertility in lactating mothers even in the early months.

Various studies have pointed to the role of the sucking stimulus in relation to lactation amenorrhea, and it has become apparent to us that the sucking stimulus is the main factor behind lactation amenorrhea.[7] We discovered that suckling is related to "natural mothering," that is, the absence of bottles, pacifier, and so on, with the mother meeting the baby's various physical and emotional needs via the breast. Natural mothering seems to provide the sucking stimulation at the breast necessary for inhibiting ovarian and menstrual activity.

A questionnaire was designed to investigate a number of variables that can influence the amount of sucking by the baby. The purpose of the study was (a) to compare amenorrhea on the basis of different types of baby care and (b) to test the following hypothesis: Mothers who breast-feed according to a system of total natural mothering will experience a period of amenorrhea that will be significantly longer than that experienced by those who breast-feed in accord with certain cultural practices (use of bottles, pacifiers, early solids, etc.).

Methods

Starting in June 1970 the questionnaire on breast-feeding experience was included in each copy of *Breastfeeding and Natural Child Spacing* by Sheila Kippley,[8] and reader-mothers were requested to complete and return it. Name and address were not requested. By June 1971 questionnaires representing 142 nursing experiences had been returned

6. Rose Gioiosa, "Breastfeeding and Child Spacing," La Leche League reprint no. 21 (no longer available).

7. Albert Sharman, "Ovulation After Pregnancy," *Fertility and Sterility* 2 (1951): 371; Thomas McKeown and J. R. Gibson, "A Note on Menstruation and Conception During Lactation," *Journal of Obstetrics and Gynecology of the British Empire* 61 (1954): 824; Hiroshi Minaguchi and Joseph Meites, "Effect of Suckling on Hypothalamic LH-Releasing Factor and Prolactin Inhibiting Factor, and on Pituitary LH and Prolactin," *Endocrinology* 80 (1967): 603; Isadore Udesky, "Ovulation in Lactating Women," *American Journal of Obstetrics and Gynecology* 59 (1950): 843; C. E. Grosvenor, F. Mena, and D. A. Schaefgen, "Effect of Nonsuckling Interval and Duration of Suckling on the Suckling-Induced Fall in Pituitary Prolactin Concentration in the Rat," *Endocrinology* 81 (1967): 449; World Health Organization, "Neuroendocrinology and Reproduction in the Human," Technical Report Series no. 304 (Geneva, 1965).

8. Cincinnati: K Publishers, 1969.

from 77 mothers. Because of insufficient data, 30 returns were eliminated. The resultant sample consisted of 112 nursing experiences, of at least four months' duration, from 72 mothers, and most of these experiences occurred prior to reading *Breastfeeding and Natural Child Spacing*.

These questionnaires were further examined to select (a) those mothers who breast-fed exclusively for at least five months and (b) those mothers who followed the approach to mothering and infant care recommended in the book mentioned above.

Length of amenorrhea was taken from the response to "How old was your baby when your periods returned?" For the statistical analysis, a response of anywhere from 1.0 to 1.9 was recorded as 1.0, thus yielding a slightly conservative bias. In those cases where amenorrhea was reestablished, we recorded amenorrhea only in terms of the first menstrual bleeding.

Results

Entire Sample

The 112 nursing experiences ranged from four to thirty-seven months of breast-feeding. (Data were not complete since some mothers stated that they were still nursing.) Table 1 indicates the distribution of this sample by months of breast-feeding; Table 2, the distribution by months of amenorrhea. This group experienced an almost equally wide range of amenorrhea—from one to thirty months.

The mean (average) months of breast-feeding was 16.3; the mean months of amenorrhea was 10.2.

Total Breast-feeding Sample

The range of one to thirty months of amenorrhea among women who were all interested enough to breast-feed from at least four months to more than three years led us to look for factors that might be significant in accounting for the difference in amenorrhea experience. Thus, we selected first of all only those cases where the mother gave no solids or liquids until the baby was at least five months old. This "total breast-feeding" group offered only mother's milk for their baby's nourishment. No juices, formula, water, or cereals and other solids were given during the total breast-feeding period.

This selection yielded seventy-five nursing experiences. Tables 3

TABLE 1. DISTRIBUTION OF ENTIRE SAMPLE BY
MONTHS OF BREAST-FEEDING [N=112 EXPERIENCES
(72 MOTHERS)]

Months of breast-feeding	Number of experiences	Percent of total experiences
4	2	1.8
5–8	14	12.5
9–12	28	25.0
13–16	23	20.6
17–20	14	12.5
21–24	12	10.7
25–28	9	8.0
29–32	6	5.3
33–36	3	2.7
37	1	0.9

Mean months of breast-feeding = 16.3
Median months of breast-feeding = 15.0

TABLE 2. DISTRIBUTION OF ENTIRE SAMPLE BY
MONTHS OF AMENORRHEA [N=112 EXPERIENCES
(72 MOTHERS)]

Months of amenorrhea	Number of experiences	Percent of total experiences
1–4	21	18.7
5–8	23	20.6
9–12	37	33.0
13–16	18	16.1
17–20	9	8.0
21–24	2	1.8
25–28	1	0.9
29–30	1	0.9

Mean months of amenorrhea = 10.2
Median months of amenorrhea = 10.0

and 4 give the results of statistical analysis, with Table 4 showing that while the range of amenorrhea experience duplicated that of the larger group, the mean average had lengthened to 11.6 months.

TABLE 3. DISTRIBUTION OF TOTAL BREAST-FEEDING SAMPLE BY MONTHS OF BREAST-FEEDING [N=75 EXPERIENCES (53 MOTHERS)]

Months of total breast-feeding	Number of experiences	Percent of total experiences
5	34	45.3
6	28	37.3
7	3	4.0
8	7	9.3
9	2	2.7
10	1	1.3

Mean months of total breast-feeding = 5.9
Median months of total breast-feeding = 6.0

TABLE 4. DISTRIBUTION OF TOTAL BREAST-FEEDING SAMPLE BY MONTHS OF AMENORRHEA [N=75 EXPERIENCES (53 MOTHERS)]

Months of amenorrhea	Number of experiences	Percent of total experiences
1–4	11	14.7
5–8	12	16.0
9–12	24	32.0
13–16	14	18.7
17–20	9	12.0
21–24	3	4.0
25–28	1	1.3
29–30	1	1.3

Mean months of amenorrhea = 11.6
Median months of amenorrhea = 12.0

Natural Mothering Sample

The third and perhaps most striking analysis was achieved by selecting only those cases that met our criteria for natural mothering, a term used to signify that type of baby care in which the baby had ample opportunity to suck at the breast for both physical and emotional nourishment. In addition to the criterion of mother-only nourishment in the early months that characterized the selection of the previous group, the criteria for this group included the exclusion of such items as pacifiers and the inclusion of certain nursing practices such as lying-down nursing. These criteria were directly related to practices that increase or decrease the sucking of the baby at the breast:

No pacifiers used
No bottles used
No solids or liquids for 5 months
No feeding schedules other than baby's
Presence of night feedings
Presence of lying-down nursing
(naps, night feedings)

Tables 5 and 6 illustrate the results of analysis of this sample. These cases ranged from twelve to thirty-seven months of breast-feeding

TABLE 5. DISTRIBUTION OF NATURAL MOTHERING
SAMPLE BY MONTHS OF BREAST-FEEDING [N=29
EXPERIENCES (22 MOTHERS)]

Months of breast-feeding	Number of experiences	Percent of total experiences
12	1	3.5
13–16	5	17.2
17–20	7	24.2
21–24	4	13.7
25–28	6	20.7
29–32	3	10.3
33–36	2	6.9
37	1	3.5

Mean months of breast-feeding=22.8
Median months of breast-feeding=23.0

(not complete, as some mothers were still nursing at date of question-naire); the mean was 22.8 months. This group experienced a sig-nificant increase in the duration of amenorrhea, with a mean of 14.6 months—an increase of 43 percent over the mean of the entire sample of 112. The range of one to thirty months of amenorrhea duplicated that of the entire questionnaire sample.

Comment

The significance of these results comes from a comparison with other studies. Pascal's[9] three-year study of 449 French (Parisian) nursing experiences (1965–1968) dealt with a group of women who did not nurse as long and who experienced a relatively short duration of amen-orrhea. In the Pascal study, only 7 percent of the babies were breast-fed for six months or more; in the present study, 98 percent of the babies were breast-fed for six months or more. Pascal's group averaged only fifty-eight days of amenorrhea, while in the present study an average amenorrhea of ten months was found. On the other hand, the present study shows that American women can have a breast-feeding–amenorrhea experience similar to that found among Asian–Indian

TABLE 6. DISTRIBUTION OF NATURAL MOTHERING SAMPLE BY MONTHS OF AMENORRHEA [N=29 EXPERIENCES (22 MOTHERS)]

Months of amenorrhea	Number of experiences	Percent of total experiences
1–4	2	6.9
5–8	2	6.9
9–12	7	24.1
13–16	9	31.0
17–20	5	17.2
21–24	2	6.9
25–28	1	3.5
29–30	1	3.5

Mean months of amenorrhea = 14.6
Median months of amenorrhea = 14.0

9. *Op. cit.*

women.[10] In other words, the difference found in previous studies has been explained in this study of a group of American women who have breast-fed according to a natural, ecologic pattern. We draw the inference that the differences are due, not to biologic differences, but to cultural practices that can be transcended by an informed mother.

The present study cannot be considered a study of breast-feeding and amenorrhea experiences from a representative sample of U.S. mothers. Rather, it is a study of mothers who were rather seriously interested in breast-feeding and the natural aspects of mothering. By selecting a subgroup of mothers who engaged in a rather full pattern of satisfying the baby's nutritional and emotional sucking needs at the breast, the study has pointed out the effect of cultural conditioning on breast-feeding–amenorrhea. Those whose breast-feeding practice was quite ecologically balanced and free from the usual cultural artifacts (such as pacifiers) and practices (such as avoiding night feedings) experienced an amenorrhea with a mean 43 percent greater than the sample as a whole. The sample as a whole showed an average duration of amenorrhea five times that of the sample in the Pascal study.

Special Notes

Analysis of the individual questionnaires revealed some interesting data not presented in the above tables.

Early Return of Menses

The woman who engaged in the natural-mothering program and yet experienced the return of menses at six weeks postpartum (one month in the tables) volunteered the information that she kept basal temperature charts. Her obstetrician interpreted these as indicating infertile periods up through the eleventh menses. The mother with a menses return four months postpartum also used basal temperature charts and indicated a return of ovulation six or seven months postpartum. These were the only two cases of menses returning prior to seven months postpartum in our sample of twenty-nine cases of natural mothering.

Conception Prior to Menses

In the entire group of 142 returned questionnaires, there were 14 instances of pregnancy occurring prior to the return of menses.

10. *Op. cit.*

(Eighty-nine of the 142 cases indicated reliance on amenorrhea for conception regulation.) Thirteen of these questionnaires provided enough detail for analysis of baby-care–feeding programs. Of these, only 2 were among the 29 who followed the program of total natural mothering. One mother conceived at twenty-seven months postpartum, but she had deliberately reduced the nursing in order to conceive; the other mother became pregnant at fifteen months postpartum. The other 11 were from the larger sample whose nursing habits were more typical of the American culture. An analysis in Table 7 indicates significant factors in their nursing or mothering patterns.

There were no conceptions by any mother in the natural mothering group of twenty-nine prior to the twelfth month, and the earliest conception without a "warning" menses was the fifteenth month, as stated above.

Conclusions

The results of this study provide further support for the statement: Ecologically natural breast-feeding effectively provides natural infertility prior to menses. "Ecologically natural" refers to the pattern described as natural mothering. What is the rate of effectiveness? Our sample indicated 100 percent effectiveness in the first year prior to menses, but we would not claim that incidence on a larger scale. Dr. Konald Prem[11] of the University of Minnesota Medical School notes that in 1895 Remfry found that the chances of pregnancy during amenorrhea were six in one hundred. Prem's own research corroborated this. On the basis of those studies plus our own, we feel warranted in saying that the mother who follows the natural-mothering program of nursing her baby will have a 95 percent probability of remaining infertile prior to the return of menses. We think, further, that U.S. women who follow the natural-mothering program will, on the average, experience twelve to sixteen months of amenorrhea. Thus, those who rely only on the natural breast-feeding program for family planning can, on the average, anticipate twenty-one to twenty-five months between births. We can make these statements, in full awareness of the many pregnancies that occur during breast-feeding, because we have limited them to cover only mothers who are willing to run contrary to the customary advice of many physicians (e.g., "start cereals at two weeks") and certain cultural practices (e.g., "let the

11. Konald Prem, "Post-Partum Ovulation" (Paper presented at La Leche League International Convention, Chicago, July 1971).

TABLE 7. ANALYSIS OF THE RELATION OF NURSING
PATTERNS TO CONCEPTION IN ELEVEN TYPICALLY
AMERICAN MOTHERS

Month of conception	Comment
2nd	Began liquids on Day 1, used pacifier
5th	Began liquids at 1 month, solids at 4 months, night feedings for only 3 months
6th	Began solids and liquids at 6 months, no night feedings, no lying-down nursing
7th	Began solids at 3 months, liquids at 6 months, night feedings for only 3 months, no lying-down nursing, nursed on a schedule
8th	Solids at 2 months, liquids at 7 months, pacifier used
8th	Weaned at 8 months, conceived before next period
9th	Totally breast-fed for 1 month, solids at 4 months (other data insufficient)
11th	Solids at 5 months (no other data)
11th	Solids at 4 months, liquids at 6 months, night feedings for 6 months, used pacifier
12th	Solids at 5 months
14th	Solids at 5 months, used bottle and pacifier, night feedings for 10 months

baby cry it out"). Those who are willing to take care of their baby's nutritional and emotional needs through breast-feeding should be specifically informed about the ecologic interdependence of mother and baby. Like many such relationships, this one has a certain delicacy, and nursing mothers who would appreciate the period of extended natural infertility deserve to know how a cultural practice such as using a pacifier can upset the balance and greatly reduce the chances of extended natural infertility.

Additional Commentary on the Survey

Sometimes a study becomes more significant in clarity and importance when seen in the light of another work. The following comparison of Pascal's[12] work with our own shows that there is a big difference in the two nursing groups as to duration of nursing and amenorrhea. In addition, it illustrates the confusion one encounters when trying to comprehend what the researcher really meant by "fully

TABLE 8. COMPARISON WITH STUDY BY JULIETTE PASCAL (SR. MARIE CHRISTINE) 1965–1968: FRANCE

		Pascal	Kippleys
Time:		3 years	1 year
N:	Total Experiences	750	112
	Mothers	509	72
	Nonbreast-feeders	301	—
	Breast-feeding experiences	449	112
	Complete breast-feeding with sudden weaning	72 (16%)	—
	Mixed breast-feeding from childbirth	100 (22%)	9 (8%)
	Complete breast-feeding with gradual weaning	277 (62%)	103 (92%)
N:	Breast-fed beyond 6 weeks	42%	100%
	Breast-fed beyond 6 months	7%	98%
Average Amenorrhea		58 days	10 months

12. *Op. cit.*

lactating" or "supplementation" and so on. Definitions are usually absent, and thus the reader is left with his own assumptions.

Pascal divided her nursing mothers into three groups: (1) total breast-feeding with sudden weaning, (2) mixed breast-feeding from childbirth, and (3) total breast-feeding with gradual weaning. I tried to arrange my nursing mothers into three similar groups. This was difficult, since her "complete breast-feeding and gradual weaning" group was 62 percent of the 449 nursing cases. By this definition one might assume that these mothers nursed for at least six months, yet only 7 percent nursed beyond six months. One then assumes that the cultural program of early solids and the use of the bottle may account for the shortened lactation among these French mothers, and that this form of nursing is associated with an early return of menstruation.

Note that in our study 98 percent of the mothers nursed at least 6.0 months; the entire sample averaged 16.3 months of breast-feeding. Many of our mothers did not offer solids or liquids until the baby was five or six months old. Our entire nursing sample averaged 8.0 more months of infertility than the entire Pascal nursing sample.

It was also decided to study the night feeding habits of the twenty-nine nursing babies in our "natural mothering" group mentioned earlier. From this study it became evident that nursing a one-year-old and even a two-year-old during the night was a normal pattern for these mothers. These twenty-nine babies averaged 20.8+ months of night feedings. The plus sign is used because fifteen babies were still nursing during the night at the time the survey was filled out; these fifteen babies averaged 23.9+ months of night feedings. Of the entire group of twenty-nine babies, there was a wide range as to the duration of nighttime feedings. One baby quit at six months of age while at the other end of the scale was a thirty-seven-month-old child who was still interested in nighttime nursing.

I also noticed that although the mothers were waiting a length of time before their babies took solid foods, they were introducing liquids too quickly once solids were begun. In this particular study the Rose Gioiosa plan for spacing babies was used as a standard for comparison. Her work was written up in the *American Journal of Obstetrics and Gynecology* (1955), the *Child and Family* magazine, and was made available to La Leche League mothers over the years in a reprint entitled "Breastfeeding and Child Spacing."[13] The Gioiosa plan was also chosen because many of our sample mothers were League

13. *Op. cit.*

mothers, and thus we thought they might have had some exposure to this reprint. The Gioiosa guidelines can be summed up in two parts: the mother should (1) wait about six months before giving baby solids and (2) wait nine or more months before giving the baby other liquids.

Some mothers have been confused by the above formula and what it meant. It means that the mother offers only breast milk for the first six months, then at about six months the baby begins to take solid foods. Once solids are begun, the baby continues to receive only breast milk for his liquid diet—until nine months or more when he begins gradually to sip other liquids from a cup.

Sixty-six surveys gave the following data on the following points: (1) no solids until the baby was five months old or older and (2) the time when other liquids were begun. All liquids were begun obviously after five months of age or else the mother was not totally breast-feeding for five months and thus was excluded from this sample. Of these sixty-six surveys, twenty-eight babies (42 percent) began other liquids at five to six months of age; twenty-three, or 35 percent, began other liquids at seven to eight months of age; only fifteen, or 23 percent, began other liquids at nine to fourteen months of age. Thus 77 percent began liquids prior to nine months of age. Only 23 percent of the sixty-six babies had mothers who followed the Gioiosa program.[14]

I do not want to leave the impression that babies should never be given a cup prior to nine months; that would hardly be compatible with the philosophy of baby-led weaning. Some babies will show a real desire for the cup before nine months. However, the high percentage of babies in our survey taking liquids at earlier months leads me to believe that the cup was offered too early to a good number of these babies.

Breast-feeding Survey

Despite the large number of studies about breast-feeding mothers, there has been almost no research that has dealt specifically with a group of women who were totally breast-feeding for a length of time. Some of us who are interested in breast-feeding and natural child spacing want to compile statistics on the subject. My husband and I have already completed a small study, and we want to follow up

14. Presented at the La Leche International Convention, Chicago, 1971, by the author.

with a larger study. You can help us by completing and returning this questionnaire.

You can do this in several different ways. You can use a piece of ordinary paper and write in the numbers only, followed by your responses. Or you can use a copy machine to make your own copy of the questionnaire. Or you may obtain one or more survey forms by writing Couple to Couple League P.O. Box 11084, Cincinnati, Ohio 45211. Please return all surveys to that address.

The name-address-phone information is optional. If you feel more comfortable omitting it, then leave it off. You may find some items not applicable. If so, simply answer them with "n/a." Many of the questions can be answered with a simple yes or no, and then other questions look for additional details.

1. Name _____
2. Address _____
3. Zip _____
4. Phone _____
5. Mother's age at time of the birth of the child covered in tnis survey _____
6. Number of children _____
7. Had you nursed other babies? _____
8. If so, for how long? _____
9. This survey covers baby number _____
10. Born _____
11. Did this nursing experience occur before or after reading this book? _____
12. How many months did you totally breast-feed? _____
13. How many months did you nurse your baby? _____
14. Did your baby have a pacifier? _____
15. If so, when was it first used? _____
16. How often was it used? _____
17. Did your baby have a bottle? _____
18. If so, when was it first used? _____
19. How often was it used? _____
20. Did you give your baby night feedings? _____
21. If so, for how long? _____
22. Did you nurse lying down for naps or during the night? _____
23. Did you sleep with your baby during the night? _____
24. Did you take your baby with you for trips, shopping, etc.? _____
25. At what age did you leave the baby at home? _____
26. For what reasons did you leave the baby? _____

27. For how many hours did you leave the baby? _____
28. Did you nurse the baby as often as he liked? _____
29. Did the baby like to be nursed to sleep? _____
30. Were there other times when the baby liked to be pacified at the breast? _____
31. Did you have a bottle or pacifier in the house? _____
32. Did you feed your baby by a schedule? _____
33. How old was the baby when you first gave him solids? _____
34. How old was the baby when you first gave him water or other liquids? _____
35. Did you rely on breast-feeding alone for family planning *before* a period or spotting occurred? _____
36. If you relied only on breast-feeding (and no other form of birth regulation), when did you conceive again or have you? _____
37. Did you rely on natural family-planning signs and then practice abstinence at any time during this breast-feeding experience? _____
38. If so, how old was the baby when you switched from total reliance on breast-feeding to methods of natural family planning? _____
39. Did you encourage or hasten weaning? _____
40. Did you let the baby wean himself? _____
41. How old (in months) was the baby when your period returned? _____
42. Once menstruation returned, did you miss a period or experience a long time between periods? _____
43. If yes, can you explain why? (Increased nursing, changes in mothering habits, etc.) _____
44. What was the spacing of your menstrual periods while nursing? (Give number of days between the first day of each period if you can) _____
45. Did you have any spotting—no matter how slight—before the return of your period? _____
46. If yes, when did it occur? _____
47. Do you have any idea why the spotting occurred? _____
48. Explain if possible the return of your period. (E.g., weaning) _____
49. Or was there any other possible reason for decreased nursings 2–6 weeks before the return of your periods? (E.g., baby's illness, etc.) _____

50. Did your husband give you support? _____
51. Did your doctor give you support? _____
52. What were the doctor's views on natural spacing? _____
53. Your comments are welcome here. _____

We appreciate your cooperation in completing this survey.

Appendix III

Natural Family Planning

Response to the first, mimeographed edition of *Breastfeeding and Natural Child Spacing* included many requests for further information about natural family planning. Many couples see a logical package that includes natural childbirth, natural breast-feeding, and natural family planning. My husband and I go farther and see natural family planning as the only real answer to the technological invasion of human sexuality, love, and procreation. Technological man may succeed in his efforts to separate sex and procreation completely. Technology can give freedom from the risk of pregnancy, freedom to have unlimited sexual intercourse, freedom from carrying a child for nine months, and, of course, freedom from that old-fashioned mammarian activity called breast-feeding. Whether such "freedoms" help a person develop as a human being is strongly debated by many.

Our convictions have been fortified by the realization of how the two most popular forms of technological birth control operate. At the Workshop for Marriage and Family Life Education at St. John's University in Collegeville, Minnesota, in June of 1972, Dr. Albert Lorincz explained the operation of the oral contraceptives. In answer to a direct question, he stated that we cannot say for sure that the oral contraceptive pill does not act as an abortifacient. That accords with the statement of some of the drug companies that the efficiency of the pill may be due to changes it causes in the endometrium. In other words, the effectiveness of the pill may be due to its affecting the lining of the womb so that a newly conceived human life cannot implant and therefore dies. Peel and Potts note that "breakthrough ovulation" occurs in 2 to 10 percent of cycles among oral contraceptive users, making the other actions of the pill quite important. Some "render the cervical mucus hostile to sperm." Others would achieve their effect in an abortifacient manner, for "it seems likely that the uterine epithelium of a woman taking a serial oral contraceptive is also unsuitable for receiving the fertilized egg even if ovulation and fertilization have taken place."[1]

At the same workshop, Dr. Tom Hilgers reported on the results of reviewing over four hundred medical articles on the operation of the IUD. He noted that the evidence was overwhelming that the IUD acted against the already conceived life and was therefore an abortifacient.

Quite obviously, the philosophy in back of this book is one of fostering infants' rights to love, care, and the best nutrition. We are only being consistent when we shrink from any method of family planning that would kill a human being even if he is only a few days old and not yet securely settled in his mother's womb.

While we acknowledge that there are many who apparently look for man's technology to give us a better way of doing things than God supplied in the natural ways, we choose to disagree. To assist people who think along similar lines, this book on breast-feeding has been written.

Just as there has been much ignorance about breast-feeding both in general and with special reference to natural child spacing, so is there much ignorance about natural family planning. It is said it is not reliable. That is a half truth. Couples who are ill informed or who choose to ignore the signs of fertility will have unforeseen pregnancies, but for couples who are well informed and who live by what they know, natural family planning is highly effective and reliable. Furthermore, our correspondence indicates that couples have found their marriage enriched when they switched from contraception to natural family planning.

Of particular importance for the nursing mother in this regard is the observation of cervical mucus. As we noted in an earlier chapter, the available evidence indicates that about 94 percent of nursing mothers will not become pregnant prior to the return of menstruation. To find out if she is in that other small group for whom fertility comes before the first menses, the nursing mother can examine herself for cervical mucus. This mucus is part of nature's preparation for pregnancy as it aids sperm life and migration. In *The Art of Natural Family*

1. John Peel and Malcolm Potts, M.D., *The Textbook of Contraceptive Practice* (New York: Cambridge University Press, 1969), p. 98.

Planning[2] my husband and I must describe how this mucus changes in consistency and how this is related to the "rules of the game" for natural family planning. Suffice it to say that the well-informed mother can detect the onset of ovulation even before the first menstruation. Furthermore, she can nurse as long as she and the baby desire and still practice natural family planning successfully.

2. Available through Couple to Couple League, P.O. Box 11084, Cincinnati, Ohio 45211.

Appendix IV

Of Babies, Beds and Teddy Bears

by James Kenny and Robert Schreiter

"It is crazy what some of these communes are doing. There is a big Esalen community here in Monterey that this friend of mine has been going to and thinks is so great. Do you realize they bathe in the nude together!! Thank goodness I don't understand it all, but my opinion is they are all nuts. They are trying to get attuned again to feeling and touching. What is happening in this world today? Is everyone going crazy? You mean to tell me people have to *learn* how to feel and touch! Where is old-fashioned common sense?"

Thus did one California resident evaluate sensitivity groups. Much of their popularity (and also of the criticism they incur) comes from their emphasis on contact, honest-to-goodness physical contact. Some see it as too intimate; others go further and say it is too sexy. Probably all would agree that human beings, adults as well as children, have a natural urge to be sociable and cuddle. Yet most adults find touch a problem. They will twist and turn in contortions worthy of a gymnast or ballerina just to avoid brushing against someone on the street. Touching is taboo.

For many, the separation from close physical contact begins right after birth. Sleeping alone in one's bed, even alone in one's own room, seems to be getting more and more common in America. The newborn infant is placed in a bassinette and generally in another room. This is so that the parents, especially the father, will not be disturbed by the baby's crying or alarmed by its strange breathing habits. Yet anthropologist Whiting tells us that this practice is not universal or even usual. In 48 of 56 societies studied, a baby slept in the same bed with its mother for at least a year after birth. In half these societies the baby slept between mother and father.

Whatever else it is, birth is certainly a change of scene. Gone is the warm, dark, quiet, and watery environment. Gone is the condition of total envelopment, the mild pressure, and the rhythmical physical "touch" that is experienced in the womb. Gone is the mother's constant and total caress. One obvious way of making the newborn feel at home in its new environment would be to continue this prenatal pattern of contact as much as possible. More simply, this would mean that good mothering means much holding and cuddling of the baby.

There are several psychological studies which support cuddling.

Holding and Crying

The more babies were held, the less they cried. Psychologists Ourth and Brown found that babies who were held three to four times longer while being fed, cried less than those who were held briefly. This simply confirms what every parent knows, that if you want to quiet the baby, you put him on your shoulder and walk him. The touch of being held and the physical rhythm of walking seem to reassure him.

Other psychologists have studied infant animals. The most famous of such studies are Harlow's experiments with monkeys. He placed newborn monkeys in separate, isolated cages, each with two mother-substitutes. One "mother" was made of wire but had bottles of milk where a monkey mother's breasts and nipples would be. The other "mother" was made of terry cloth. Harlow found that the little monkeys would leave food and warmth to cling to the cloth mother most of the day, especially when they were afraid. He also found that monkeys raised without a real mother were not as adults able to develop the full and normal patterns of affection. They were unable to socialize and unable to mate. Harlow's conclusion: love derives mainly from close bodily contact in the early months of life.

In a later study Harlow found that physical contact with infant brothers and sisters could compensate for the lack of contact with the mother. Infant monkeys raised together, but without a real mother, grew up capable of adult relationships. Much of their infant contact was rough-and-tumble play, with jumping, scuffling, wrestling, hair-pulling, and a little nipping thrown in. It sounds like bedtime in the old-fashioned large family. In any case, the comfort obtained from contact or touch includes a lot more than affectionate snuggling. In a recent article on the nature of love, Harlow concluded that for infants love is defined in terms of body contact, warmth, and rocking motion.

Along with the ability to sense warmth and cold, the sense of touch is present and well-developed in the human being at birth. The sense of pain will not come for a few weeks. Taste, smell, hearing, and vision are present, but only on a very rudimentary level. It will be several years before the many fine discriminations involved in hearing and vision can be mastered, before the child receives information through these senses that has much meaning.

Our senses are the channels through which we can know about the world. For example, think of the many ways that the world can communicate "I love you" to us. Most obviously, someone can simply tell us so. But wearing perfume for us may say as much. Or a smile. Or feeding us. Or a caress and a squeeze. The problem with being an infant is that the channels for receiving meaningful information are limited. Most messages from the world to the newborn baby need to be sent on the tactile channel, the sense of touch. One very nice feature of breast-feeding is that no other act so effectively guarantees intimate bodily contact between mother and child. It is an interesting side note that 70 percent of successful breast-feeding mothers also take their babies to bed with them.

Tactile stimulation awakens the baby's first personal responses to the world. Touching, particularly on the cheeks and lips, awakens responses of the mouth, head, and neck. These responses are not learned, nor do they depend on his being hungry or cold; they come naturally—in response to being touched.

Primitive Sense

The sense of touch is perhaps the most primitive of all our senses. It is comprised of nerve endings which respond to mechanical energy. Other senses are more complex and more specialized. Some respond to thermal energy; others, to chemical and electromagnetic energy. Yet there are biologists who say that these more complicated receptors have evolved from the sense of touch. It is both the source and the basic underpinning of our other senses. In fact, without internal touch, without the possibility of our internal organs communicating with one another through pressure, we would die within minutes.

The tactile sense is all the more important for infants because contact between the infant and its world is so limited. Watch a baby wave its arms, kick its feet, flail out at a world it cannot talk to, a world it cannot see very well—but a world it can touch. It seems a near-desperate attempt to reach the world.

184

Life itself may be dependent on touch. Studies by Spitz have shown that a lack of mothering can raise the rate of infant mortality. Babies left alone in their cribs and cubicles except for feeding and diapering had a much higher death rate than those who were handled more often. In one specific, but typical, instance the infant mortality rate rose alarmingly among children being kept in a hospital awaiting adoption. Extra precautions were taken to ensure that these chidren would not be exposed to dirt or contagion; nutrition was adequate to good; but the death rate continued to climb. Finally, one of the physicians decided that the only remaining difference between these babies and the "normal" babies was that the pre-adoptive babies were getting less "mothering." They were being handled less. So the "love bank" was begun, a group of volunteer mothers who came into the hospital daily to handle and hold, cradle and coo at, their foster infants. The mortality rate returned to normal. The physicians concluded that the problem had been a lack of TLC (tender loving care). This same cycle has been repeated at other hospitals and institutions.

Mental health has also been affected by what is referred to as early "maternal deprivation." Studies by Bowlby, Stone, Rheingold, and others have related lack of mothering to symptoms of increased irritability, lack of appetite, excessive dependence, increased aversion to strangers, delayed speech, and depressed intelligence. Unfortunately, in some of these studies, no clear operational definition of maternal deprivation is given. However, when the basic needs for food, warmth, and cleanliness are met, it is hard to imagine what else maternal deprivation could mean except less frequent physical contact.

Support for man's need for social contact has come from sensory deprivation experiments. Psychologists concerned about the effects of space travel have asked the question: What happens to man if we close down his senses, his sources of contact with the outside world? We know that most prisoners kept too long in solitary confinement become temporarily insane, sometimes suffering from hallucinations. But what about normal people? Suppose we put stoppers in their noses and ears, cover their eyes, stretch out their arms and legs so that they cannot touch themselves; immerse them in water of a moderate temperature—in general, cut off communication with the outside world. Such experiments have been attempted. What happens? Most adults are unable to tolerate this isolation. There is a progressive and rather rapid breakdown of contact with reality; disorganized thinking and behavior emerge. It seems that human beings need the constant stimulation of contact with the "outside world."

A Blank Past

Now what about infants? Infants do not have the large memory store of past experiences to regurgitate and think about when no new information is coming in. The past is somewhat of a blank. No images to call up. So when nothing new is coming in, the situation must be even more serious. Add to this the fact that the infant's information-receiving equipment is still very limited, and you can see the importance of touch. Babies need the comfort of lots of affectionate handling and contact. Flesh on flesh—or at least terry cloth.

Running counter to this need for bodily contact is a modern trend toward sleeping alone. Isolated sleeping rooms and beds are a relatively new phenomenon in human history. In the sixteenth century in England it was common for the more wealthy people to have extremely large beds—large enough for the whole household to sleep in them. The so-called Trinity bed developed during this time. It consisted of a large bed upon which the immediate family slept, and two smaller beds that rolled out from underneath the larger bed. Here the servants and more distant relatives slept. In the seventeenth century perhaps the largest of all beds was designed by John Fosbrooke for the royal family. It could sleep 102 persons! From this it can be seen that individual beds were certainly not a sign of affluence in England.

Sleeping together was quite common and accepted in early America, according to Calhoun, even among the sex-conscious Puritans. Since there was usually only one bed in the house, any visitor staying overnight would crawl right in with the rest of the family. This was allowed even if the husband were away and the wife were the only one home. It was simply a matter of hospitality. Calhoun records from Martha Washington's diary how she often slept with strangers while George was away. Martha mentions this very matter-of-factly. Not just sleeping, but much cold-weather visiting was done in bed. This was the custom of bundling. Because of the lack of heat in the house, callers usually conversed with their hosts in bed. This included young men who came to call upon ladies. The custom persisted until after the French and Indian War, when it seems that both young men and, therefore, bundling lost that innocence they had previously enjoyed.

Then Single Beds

Double beds continued to be part of the American scene until the 1920s, when the use of single beds became widespread. The exact origin of single or twin beds is not clear. The reason most often given for the change is "hygiene," although the exact type of hygiene desired is rarely mentioned. Eckersall cites the information, based on the studies of sleeping patterns of individuals, that every person needs an absolute minimum of thirty-nine inches to flounder around in. For the sake of a good night's sleep, the individual bed is the best thing. Since this idea arose from medical advice, the factor of communicable diseases may have played a part in the switch to single beds.

But children are very adaptable creatures. Isolated in separate rooms, placed in a single bed, what do they do? They take toys to bed with them. Gesell notes this as common from eighteen months to seven years. The teddy bear (or security blanket) is a common bedtime companion. The teddy bear, with his furry, ruffly-textured coat, provides considerable tactile sensation. Teddy is lovable, pleasurable. He is a source of security. Especially under the stress of fear, he provides a chance to get in "touch" with a loving and safe world. "I will take care of you," the snuggle may say to the child.

Fear of the dark is very prevalent in childhood, from age two until almost age eight. Darkness shrouds the normal visual and depth-perception cues that give the child his orientation within the environment. These cues vanish with sundown or lights-out. Not only do cues for the environment vanish, but even the child's own body vanishes, making him as invisible as the rest of the world. This situation produces anxiety. The child is left with only sound and touch. But severing the visual from the auditory sense, sight from hearing, causes a great deal of anxiety. It seems that during light-hours the child attends more to sight than to hearing; he understands sound stimuli only in reference to a seen object. Hence in the dark he has trouble connecting noises with their visual source. With the world of sight gone, the child is left with the world of sound—the world of wind, animal noises, and sirens— a world he would not attend to during the day. To make matters worse, the child is often "privileged" with his own room and confined in his own bed. This means no older person is there to reassure or protect him against the things that go bump in the night. But even the presence of another person in the room may not be enough. Usually children end up by scurrying into bed with the other person. Why? When darkness has taken sight, when sound is threatening, then touch is all that's left. It is a return to a period when things were not so threatening, when being curled up in the womb was a way of life. The child will move in with whoever is closest—preferably the parents, although an older brother or sister will do.

But then, this should not strike adults as so strange. We might ask how it is that most human mating takes place in bed, in the dark. Very few other species limit their lovemaking to night—or equate sex and sleeping. To "sleep with" has become a euphemism for sexual intercourse. Perhaps we adults need to touch "Teddy" to reassure us that we are whole and the world is stable and all is well. Lovemaking was a rather happy choice—a bit of intimate snuggling and cuddling to defend against the lonely dark.

Today it is "the thing" for adults who can't relate to try group therapy. Sensitivity groups have become popular from coast to coast. One point of disagreement among the various groups is whether the persons in them should learn to touch one another physically. In one style of sensitivity training, the persons are not allowed to talk or even look, but must communicate through touch. This is very, very difficult for most American adults. One reason, I believe, is that our physical isolation from one another has been plotted since infancy. Single beds. Separate rooms. Stop fighting. Don't touch.

Appendix V

A Postscript to Husbands

by John F. Kippley

If you are a typical husband, you may not share your wife's enthusiasm for reading books and other literature about breast-feeding. Perhaps your wife will have given you this chapter and asked you to read it, so I'll make it brief. I'm just going to share a few thoughts that you might find helpful.

First of all, you can be proud of your wife for breast-feeding your baby. She's doing what is best for him—and for her. Give her support because she needs it from you. She needs to know that you are grateful she's doing what is best for the baby.

Secondly, there are some experiences that you will probably miss, or at least have less of, than the fathers of bottle-fed babies. For one thing if your wife has a prepared, natural childbirth and comes right home from the hospital, you won't have the experience of visiting her at the hospital each day for several days. Then, because a breast-fed baby has health advantages over a bottle-fed baby, your baby will most likely have fewer illnesses, allergies, and so on than if your wife had not nursed. You are also going to miss the experience of the horrible mess that is made when mothers (or fathers) try to feed babies solids in the early months. I can still distinctly remember one Saturday morning back in my bachelor days when I stopped to pick up a buddy for golf. He invited me in for a cup of coffee while his wife was feeding a very young baby. I swear that seeing that stuff all over everything—hair, face, arms—scared me into a few more years of bachelorhood. It's an experience I haven't missed at all with our breast-fed children. From the above, it is also obvious that you are going to miss the expenses associated with baby foods and medical problems.

One thing we have had some questions on is the idea of the baby sleeping in bed with his parents. We have been told of husbands who initiated the idea, and we have also heard from wives telling us that they think their husbands would object to having the baby as sort of an intruder in the marriage bed, that the presence of the baby will interfere with marital intimacy. The most simple answer is that it doesn't. "Sleeping with baby" doesn't mean he's with you all the time. He will normally be asleep before you go to bed, and you can put him in another bed for a while. I'm sure that any couple with a little ingenuity can have their marital intimacy and their "sleeping with baby," too.

Keep in mind that it is the baby's *regular* sucking that brings about breast-feeding's side effect of extended natural infertility. If you train the baby to sleep by himself all through the night, your wife may very well be deprived of the sucking stimulus her body needs for continued natural infertility and maybe even for her continued ample milk supply. It also helps to keep in mind that those night nursings are saving you the trouble of getting up for middle-of-the-night bottle warmings.

Being a father calls for a little maturity. The baby is your child, and his needs call for more instant satisfaction than yours. If your wife is preparing dinner and the baby really needs to nurse, don't get upset if dinner is a few minutes late. Don't be afraid to pitch in with the dishes when your baby needs his mother. And finally, when all that your baby needs is some holding, some walking, or some rocking, be sure to get in on the act. There is something satisfying about having your babe fall asleep in your arms.

Support your wife when she allows your child to wean at his own pace. You thought he would never walk—and then he did. You thought he would never talk—and then he did and won't stop. You think he's never going to wean—and he will when he's ready. In other cultures throughout the world it is common for three-year-olds to still nurse occasionally. Your child will be big, and older, before you know what has happened. Relax and enjoy the nursing years, and you'll be glad you did.

Appendix VI

Summary of Natural Mothering, Breast-feeding and Child Spacing Program

Basic Principles

1. The sucking stimulation by baby at the breast when repetitious and frequent inhibits the menstrual cycles.

2. Natural mothering almost always provides this adequate stimulation. By natural mothering, we mean that type of baby care which follows the natural ecology of the mother-baby relationship. It avoids the use of artifacts and follows the baby-initiated patterns. It is characterized by the items in phases I and II below.

Phase I of Natural Mothering (Mother Only)

This phase almost invariably produces infertility as long as the program is complete. What's in the program?

Use of the breast for pacification

Frequent nursing

Sleeping with baby (night feedings)

Absence of schedules

Absence of bottles or pacifiers or cups

Absence of any practice that tends to restrict nursing or separate mother and baby

Total breast-feeding in the early months

Phase II of Natural Mothering (Mother Plus Other Sources)

Begins when baby starts taking solids from the regular table.

Liquids are begun later—again when baby begins to show an interest in the cup.

Continues over a period of a year or two or more until baby gradually loses interest in nursing.

Includes what may be a long period when the baby will be nursing much more for emotional than nutritional nourishment.

Phase II is a very gradual program in which the **amount of nursing** is (1) not decreased at all at first and (2) lessened only gradually at baby's pace. Phase II begins as soon as baby receives **any** food or liquid other than mother's milk. Frequently Phase II will be longer than Phase I with regard to natural infertility **if** the natural-mothering program is followed.

Risk of Pregnancy

For the nursing mother there is a risk (about 6 percent) of pregnancy occurring prior to the first menses. This risk is reduced by the nursing mother learning to observe the mucous signs that occur several days before ovulation.

Natural Spacing by Breast-feeding Alone

For those couples who desire eighteen to thirty months between the births of their children, "natural mothering" should be sufficient.

Index

Toni S. Gould

HOME GUIDE TO EARLY READING

For the average or the bright child, preschool reading will make kindergarten and the first grade that much more rewarding; for the child who may have a learning disability, an early start is probably the only way to avoid the ordeal of later remedial instruction. Based on years of successful application by parents and teachers, Toni Gould's approach emphasizes the relationship between letters and their sounds, a method that enables the child to figure out words on his own from the start without depending on rote memorization. A reading consultant for twenty-five years, the author presents short learning games and activities that are fun for parent and child and will lead the youngster to independent discovery. A parent willing to give ten or fifteen minutes a day to this program will discover that children enjoy learning to read when the experience challenges their minds, when they understand, not memorize, each step in the process.

Gail Sforza Brewer with Tom Brewer, M.D.,
Medical Consultant

**WHAT EVERY PREGNANT WOMAN
SHOULD KNOW**
The Truth about Diets and Drugs in Pregnancy

In years of clinical experience, obstetrician Tom
Brewer came to the conclusion that birth defects are
closely associated with weight-control diets, salt
restriction, and drugs, especially diuretics. His advice to pregnant women is simple: Eat all the nour-
ishing food you want; use salt to taste; don't worry
about gaining weight; and don't take drugs unless
it's absolutely necessary. *What Every Pregnant
Woman Should Know* includes a hundred pages of
tempting menus and recipes designed to make both
mother and unborn baby get all the high-protein,
high-nutrition foods they need.

Richard de Mille

PUT YOUR MOTHER ON THE CEILING
Children's Imagination Games

The theory of imagination is growing rapidly today. Fantasy has been vindicated from charges that it is useless or neurotic and has been recognized as an indispensable resource for normal living. "Richard de Mille's innovative contribution provides children with exercises designed to prolong and preserve their penchant for taking liberties with reality, or to help them recapture this facility if they have lost it in the process of growing up and becoming social persons"—J. P. Guilford, Department of Psychology, University of Southern California. "De Mille's own soaring imagination has produced a truly unique book and the best kind of child psychology because it puts a person in touch with the most neglected and most enjoyable parts of his children and himself"—Richard E. Farson, Western Behavioral Sciences Institute.

Sheila Kitzinger

THE EXPERIENCE OF CHILDBIRTH

"For far too many women pregnancy and birth is still something that happens to them rather than something they set out consciously and joyfully to do themselves." *The Experience of Childbirth* is written by a sociologist and ante-natal teacher—herself the mother of five children—as a complete manual of physical and emotional preparation for the expectant mother. The physiology of pregnancy, the development of the fetus, and the successive stages of labor are described in detail. Sheila Kitzinger's research and teaching focus particularly on the psychological aspects of childbearing and on the preparation of both wife and husband not only for birth but also for parenthood and marital adjustment.